HOW TO LEARN ENGLISH

FABIEN SNAUWAERT

HOW TO LEARN ENGLISH

A GUIDE TO SPEAKING ENGLISH LIKE A NATIVE SPEAKER

HOW-TO-LEARN-ENGLISH.COM

How To Learn English

ISBN-10: 1453844155
ISBN-13: 978-1453844151

Website

To get new articles and tools, visit our website,
http://www.How-To-Learn-English.com.

Introduction

How to use this book

CONGRATULATIONS!

First of all, congratulations are in order! By reading this book, you are already committing yourself to reading and learning English. This is an important first step!

Practice is the key to learning any foreign language. If you do not practice often enough, you lose what you have previously learned and making progress will seem to take forever. The goal of this book is to give you many different ways to practice your English effortlessly, while having the most fun and making the most of your time.

<u>When you are done using this book, you will understand and speak English as fluently as a native speaker.</u>

HOW TO USE THIS BOOK

This book is not meant to be just read and put back on a shelf. It is meant to be used as a reference you return to again and again. It takes you from rather basic drills, as you may have been doing at school for years, to advanced levels, such as listening to an audio book, with no text to help you; or, thinking in English and making conversation with native speakers as smoothly as you would in your mother-tongue.

As such, this book must be used as a *tool*. Come back to it often and re-read the parts you are currently working on, as well as the parts you have worked on before and should still be practicing. Applying the techniques in this book does not require much effort and should be a lot of fun from the start.

Principles

For your English practice to pay off, you need to apply the following principles:

Principle #1

Have fun practicing your English. If you are not having fun, you are not learning and you may end up quitting. English is all about communication and good communication has to be enjoyable.

One easy way to do that, a concept used throughout this book, is to have your English practice revolve around *your passions*; ensuring that you both have fun and learn interesting things, while still practicing your English.

Principle #2

Practice daily. This is much easier if you respect the first principle. People are often afraid of the time and effort it takes to learn a new skill. They are afraid they will not have enough time for other activities anymore; they are also afraid that all the time they put in will have been spent in vain, if they fail to learn the new skill.

Learning English does not take a lot of time; but it requires *regular* periods of time. Twenty minutes a day can be enough to make some major progress. The brain adapts quickly, provided it feels it is doing something important. One way to reinforce that feeling is through steady practice.

Principle #3

You do it for you. It is critical for you to know why you are learning English.

Answering "for school," "for my diploma" or "for work" is not enough. You need to know what you want to get out of it. How do you want to benefit from speaking English? Knowing why will make it all the more easier when you are in doubt, facing new issues, or spending more time on your English.

You need to come up with your own personal reason for learning English. What does it enable you to do, *specifically*, that you cannot do otherwise? Be as specific as possible. The American Dream is still very much alive. Be honest with yourself: examine why you want to speak this language. Speaking English properly opens up many opportunities. Define what it is that you want.

Making progress

First, be aware that, by respecting the previous three principles, you are never wasting your time – never, ever. If you are enjoying yourself by practicing and pursuing a personal goal, how could you be?!

Still – and this is all very natural – people want to learn quickly. I think this in order to enjoy the momentum coming from their high motivation before it vanishes, and because they fear they will give things up if it takes too long.

One way to learn efficiently is to keep yourself on your toes in order to avoid both boredom and frustration.

If the task is too difficult, you will grow bored and may even resent the language…

If you feel things are too easy, you may grow bored and perhaps even disinterested.

This means you need to maintain balance in your practice. As soon as something becomes too easy, move on. As soon as something seems awfully hard slow down, and break the task into smaller pieces.

When you have learned something new and it is starting to become easy, it is okay for you to enjoy your new skills and keep doing the same thing for a while. This will only reinforce your new skills. However, you need to be aware of how things are evolving: are you feeling bored at some point? If so, move on to something more challenging. Speaking perfect English is further down the road so why wait? Usually, in practice this will mean moving on from one chapter to the next.

On the other end of the spectrum, when something gets too difficult, you need to slow down and think about it. You do not always need to go back to something easier. Maybe you just need to break down the problem into smaller pieces. What does that mean? It means (and this is *your responsibility*, as a learner) that you may need to locate what is causing you trouble. What is the difficulty, exactly? Grammar? Vocabulary? Pronunciation? Identify your stumbling block and break it into pieces. Any problem can be solved if broken down into smaller, simpler chunks. You then need to handle each piece of the puzzle separately. When they all make sense, try it again; it should then be much easier.

PRACTICE TIME

Practice at least 20 minutes per day. If you are having fun it will be very easy to increase to an hour or more each day, without noticing.

The goal is not for you to count how many hours you spend learning English. The goal is to make practicing English part of your daily routine... something as natural to you as drinking water, chatting with a friend or eating...a life-long habit.

As much as possible, and more so than any other language-learning method available, this book helps you make English part of your normal life. You will be able to add more and more English to your day without having to sacrifice something you like for it. By the end of this book, you will be doing a lot of activities you already enjoy doing, except that you will be doing them in English, instead of your native language.

A final word on practice: if you do not feel you are practicing enough, do not let it get you down. We all have tight schedules. Just do the best you can. Do remember one thing though: it is more interesting to practice twenty minutes per day, five days a week, than it is to practice two hours per week over the weekend. You need to feel that English is part of your routine; not something you only do once in a while. It actually takes **much less** effort to practice this way and you will progress **much faster**.

MY STORY

Who am I to tell you how to learn English properly?

Well, I started learning English at school like most people. One thing to mention is that I am French and that I did not study to become an English teacher. French people actually have one of the worst reputations regarding foreign languages: we hardly practice any spoken English in class. We are very proud of our French culture, which is okay in itself but prevents us from opening up to foreign languages, especially English. We do not dare speak English with foreigners, even when we know what to say, simply because we are so self-conscious of our thick French accent. So, let's just say that being French awards no extra perks in learning English. Moreover, I don't have any English-speaking relatives so I have had to learn the hard way.

Where I've been lucky is that I really wanted to learn English. I was not sure why at first, but it became obvious that I saw being able to speak English properly as an opportunity. I have been through various stages as a learner: from getting terrible grades despite my efforts; to doing the least amount of effort; to trying to get things going, and actually learning a lot... on topics I loved – that were only available in English back then. I also found out the hard way, quite a few times, that, even though I had a lot of vocabulary (at last!) I was still *not* able to get people to understand me when I spoke with them, either in person or on the phone. Let us just say that I have been through quite a few frustrations before I could speak English properly and, later on, as smoothly as my native language.

Through trial and error, I did uncover quite a few things that worked. The principles are mentioned above and the concrete applications are described in this book. At the core of it all, is the fact that learning English has to be fun. What I mean by "fun" is that what we do must be something pretty interesting, full of life, something we want to talk and think about. You quite simply do not learn English in textbooks. You only can learn grammar in those. What you will learn in this method is how to get out of the classroom and actually practice English in a fun, appealing, and modern way.

I spent literally years discovering all this material by myself. I then wrote a book in French to describe my findings that has helped hundreds of people improve their English ever since. What I would like you to keep in mind is that if a regular kid from France can become bilingual using this method, so can you.

SCHEDULE

Please use the schedule on the next page to organize your English practice. This will help you reach your goals.

The best thing to do is to place a copy of it somewhere where you can view it every day, such as in front of your desk or on a mirror.

The chapters build on one another. As such, you should practice them in sequence, in the order they appear in the book.

CONTACT

You are not alone! As you keep practicing this book, please tell me about your comments, questions and success stories.

E-mail me at this address:

fabien.snauwaert@gmail.com

Success stories are read first and I reply to everyone.

Chapter and Goal	Duration
1. Music, songs & lyrics. Practice English again and get used to it.	1–2 weeks
2. Internet tools. Learn how to learn quickly and easily.	1–2 days
3. Making friends online. Be active: find your words and express yourself.	Self-paced: 1–2 weeks Real-time: 1–2 weeks
4. Virtual Worlds. Learn visually, interact, and chat.	2 weeks
5. Accent Training. Know all the English sounds: hear them and pronounce them.	3 days
6. Reading. Finish your first books: be proud of yourself and learn a lot of vocabulary.	Novel: 1–2 weeks How-to book: 1–2 weeks
7. TV. Feel confident watching TV without subtitles and practice your English daily.	2–8 months
8. Audio Books. Hear English every day and start thinking in English.	2 weeks
9. Meeting people for fun and at work. Feel comfortable practicing with native speakers regularly.	2 months
10. Thinking in English. Think In English as naturally as in your native language.	1–3 months
TOTAL To gain a lot of experience, speak English fluently and think in English.	6–14 months

Introduction

Chapter 1

Music, songs & lyrics

In the mood for English

"Words make you think a thought.
Music makes you feel a feeling.
A song makes you feel a thought."
– E.Y. Harburg, composer

GOAL & EXIT

Goal

The goal in this chapter is to get you practicing English again. No hassle, no stress. Your mission here is just to have a good time practicing and get used to hearing English again.

In order to do so, we will be using music, songs, and lyrics.

If you have not practiced your English in awhile, now is the chance to check your basics again: grammar, vocabulary, and pronunciation. On the contrary, if you have never lost the habit of practicing your English, you may want to skim through this chapter.

Exit

Do not wait until you perfectly understand the lyrics of any song you hear before moving on to the next chapter! As soon as you feel you have shaken the rust off of your English-speaking abilities, move on to the next chapter.

ENGLISH SONGS: QUITE AN ASSET

One thing I've noticed, time and time again, is that people who were quite good in English at school had usually one thing in common: they *loved* English music. It is not just that they liked listening to the music: they also had an urge to understand what the lyrics actually meant.

This is great practice because you then get to learn vocabulary in context. Learning new words does not only mean understanding them. Learning new words means knowing how to use them, having a story around those words. Songs provide us with such a story.

What's more, the very nature of music provides one additional dimension: the mood, the feelings provided by the song. By linking words to meanings, stories and feelings, all at the same time, we increase our chance to recall later on what we heard.

Finally, everybody loves music and this makes it the easiest content with which to start our practice.

WHERE TO FIND LYRICS

You most certainly have websites in your native language where you can find your favorite lyrics. The best thing to do, however, is to not use them and instead, to exclusively use 100% English-speaking websites. This is our way to get closer to the real thing, to real English, and will make it easier to think in English (and hence speak English) later on. So, for this chapter, as well as all throughout the book, please use websites that are 100% in English.

Lyrics are pretty easy to find on the Web nowadays. Please refer to the vocabulary section later in this chapter if you need help finding them through a Web search. For now, I would like to introduce you to a few handy tools.

Lyrics software

Lyrics software loads automatically when you start the music player on your computer, and displays the lyrics of the song currently playing. This is most useful if you listen to music on your computer directly (CD or MP3). You have two main options here:

Evil Lyrics

EvilLyrics [http://www.evillabs.sk/evillyrics/] is most likely the most famous one. This works with a number of music players, including iTunes.

Lyrics Plugin

Lyrics Plugin [http://www.lyricsplugin.com] has a much nicer interface than the previous software but only works with WinAmp and Windows Media Player.

Music and lyrics on the Web

The number of free websites that allow you to legally listen to music streamed over the Web has increased over the last two years. Here are a few recommendations:

Deezer

On Deezer [http://www.deezer.com], there is a huge quantity of songs available. You can find pretty much anything. The only limitation is that the availability of titles varies from country to country; hence, you may not always be able to listen to the songs you would like, depending on where you live. Try it and see what it is like using it from your country.

YouTube

YouTube [http://www.youtube.com] is an obvious choice. The sound quality may not always be great, but if the song has a music video, you can be sure it is on YouTube.

Last.fm

Last.fm [http://www.last.fm] is great for discovering new music similar to what you already like. Just listen to your favorite songs there and see the recommendations.

Spotify

Spotify is actually a piece of software you need to install on your computer. It then lets you listen to streaming music, similar to what one can do with Deezer. There too, the list of titles available varies depending on the country you reside in.

VOCABULARY

Here are a few words related to music.

Music, songs and lyrics

Lyrics are the words of a song. *"The Beach Boys have very melancholic lyrics."*

A **song** is a piece of music made for singing. *"That song is in Ab ("A-flat")."*

A **record** is a sound recording, such as a disk to be played on a phonograph. *"Michael Jackson was awarded his first gold record for the album Thriller."*

A **track** is a sound recording, usually of a song. *"Put the next track on the CD please!"*

An **LP** (for "Long-Playing" record) is a type of vinyl record. This is usually used, however, as another word for "album". *"Eminem's new LP is out on Monday!"*

PRACTICE

The idea here is to get you listening to various songs in the coming days and weeks and make sure you get the most out of them. We will focus on one song at a time.

Choosing the song

Pick a song that you already know and like. You do not need to know the lyrics by heart but you should know the song well enough; this should be one of your favorites.

Preferably, do not pick any song with slang in it. If you like rap a lot, you might need to pick a song in a different genre to start with. If you insist on using a song with slang in it, make sure you know what the slang means. When you first start, you might not know what slang actually looks like, so just keep away from rap songs and use something where they speak slowly and clearly.

Understanding the song

Your goal here is to understand every part of the song.

❶ Text

Read the lyrics once: just the lyrics, no music for now. This is so you know the text. Next, read through the lyrics again, this time, while listening to the music. The goal here is for you to get a basic idea of how to pronounce the words.

❷ Pronunciation

Read the text again, this time, without the music, and try to pronounce the lyrics. Your goal is to focus on the words so you are able to pronounce them correctly. Put the song back on, once in a while, to check your pronunciation. Alternate between pronouncing the lyrics and listening to them, to ensure you are doing it right.

Go as slowly as possible. At this point, it is okay if you do not know the meaning of the lyrics: your goal is to open your *ears* and be able to reproduce what you hear.

Once you know the lyrics well enough (what they are and how to pronounce them), proceed to the next step

❸ Meaning

Now, check your resources (dictionary, translator) as to what the words mean. (We will see fast ways to check and remember the meaning of a word in the next chapter; for now, do as you are used to). Proceed as follows:

- Read the lyrics, one sentence at a time.
- When facing a word you do not know, check it with your dictionary or translator.
- Try to *picture* the meaning of the word in your mind. If you know the translation in your native language, see what the word evokes to you: what picture do you see, in your mind, when you think of the word?
- When reading the lyrics again, *picture* the meaning in your mind again and try to hear the *pronunciation* in your mind, both at the same time.

Examples:

- If the song you are working on is "Stairway to Heaven," when you read the words "Stairway to Heaven," you might picture in your mind's eye a series of steps (stairway) that lead to clouds (Heaven), for example; and you should hear the correct pronunciation also. When you read "All that glitters is gold," you might picture a sparkling gold bar or something similar, along with the pronunciation again.
- If you are working on the song "Thriller," when you read "the beast about to strike," you would picture a werewolf, a vampire, or anything similar (the beast), moving and about to hit something (strike); again, you should hear the proper pronunciation mentally at the same time.

I am talking about picturing things because most of us are visually oriented. You could also imagine a feeling (touch or emotions), a sound or even a smell, depending on the vocabulary. The main point is that you need to *link* these words to something in your mind. This will help your memory. More on this later.

Hearing it right

As you practice the method described in this chapter, you may have doubts about how a word is supposed to be pronounced. As you compare the pronunciation in the song to how you *thought* it was pronounced, you may observe major differences! You may even have a hard time hearing the lyrics properly at times, not able to differentiate a syllable from the next. Just keep in mind that it is okay for now. This is actually pretty normal, as you have been trained to hear things a certain way your whole life, a way that is based on your native language. For now, do your best. We will cover phonetics and pronunciation in later chapters.

Most importantly, for now, trust the words you hear over the text you read. English is more about sound than about text. Even though it may sometimes surprise you, mimic the words you hear in the actual song. Your ears will open up gradually with time.

Using this on the long-run

You should move on to the next chapter once you know the meaning of every word of at least one song. No need to do plenty of songs for now; we all listen to music often enough to get back to this practice later on.

The core idea, to get the most out of this habit, is to remember your song's lyrics throughout the day. Think about them as you are doing something else, I do not care if this is while you do your dishes or wait for the bus or whatever; just make sure that you think of them during the day. Think of them again the next day and for the next few days. Do that again, for the same song, two weeks later. As you do so each time, remember the words – what they mean (the mental pictures) and how they are pronounced (you can sing mentally or out loud). By doing so, you will remember the vocabulary from the song forever.

Our memory works in such a way that if you memorize something one day, recall it for the next few days, and then recall it again about two weeks later: you will then remember it forever. This works for lyrics; this works for anything else.

Once you have applied this technique to at least one song and remember it properly (words, pronunciation, meaning/pictures), you can move on to the next chapter.

Repeat this technique with various songs, week after week, as you practice the other methods presented in this book.

WRAPPING IT UP

❖ Get the lyrics for one of your favorite songs.

❖ Listen to the lyrics. Speak them or even *sing* them to get the words in your mouth.

❖ Break down the meaning of the lyrics word after word. Remember what the words mean: *picture* that meaning in your mind.

❖ Check the song again the next day and for the next few days. Check again two weeks later. You will now know all the vocabulary in that song perfectly.

How To Learn English

Chapter 2

Internet Tools

Learning rapidly and easily

"Give a man a fish and you feed him for a day.
Teach a man to fish and you feed him for a lifetime."
– Chinese Proverb

"Give a man a fish and you feed him for a day.
Teach him to use the Internet and he won't bother you for
weeks!"
– Internet Proverb

GOAL & EXIT

Goal

Make learning *easy* and *fast*. To do that, you will acquire *tools* enabling you to quickly grasp meanings and memorize words. You will also discover *content* you can use to quickly and easily investigate specific topics. In so doing, you will become more comfortable using the Internet in English, making the world's largest resource readily available to you.

Exit

The techniques described in this chapter will make your life *much* easier for the rest of this book and to learn English in general. As such, you should master them and make them part of your daily life.

Make sure you use the tips given in this chapter for at least a week, in order to make them easy to use and get in the habit of using them.

WWW: A NUMBERS GAME

The Web (originally WWW, for "World Wide Web"), the world's largest language resource, is at your disposal. You can quickly find a lot of free information. You already know that in your native language. Almost half of all websites are in English and there are 5 to 10 times more web pages in English than there are in major languages such as Spanish, Japanese, German or Arabic.

This means that using the Web in English is not just a good opportunity to practice your English: this also gives you an edge by making so much more information and tools available to you. Besides having more options, the content is up-to-date.

We will use these resources to increase our knowledge in general, and to improve our English skills in particular.

TOOLS

Online Dictionaries

Having a good dictionary at your disposal is critical to learn English quickly and easily. The best thing to use is an English-English dictionary. This way, you get in the habit of learning in English, avoiding the pitfall of translating in your head (bad habit, more on this later). In so doing, you start to get into the habit of *thinking* in English.

A good dictionary will also provide the pronunciation – phonetic transcriptions of the words using the International Phonetics Alphabet, as well as audio files you can listen to.

TheFreeDictionary

TheFreeDictionary [http://www.thefreedictionary.com] provides all of the above. It is here to stay. Anytime you have doubts regarding a word, I recommend you to lookup the word on TheFreeDictionary.

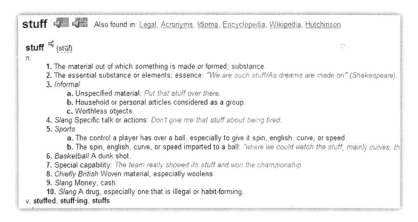

TheFreeDictoinary extensions are available for free for FireFox and Internet Explorer, so that you can look up a word quickly from any web page.

Slang dictionaries

Sometimes, you need to know about words you will not find in your typical dictionary. This is called *slang*. This is how people talk casually – be it among friends or families (usually, they do not use the same words in both groups!).

Urban Dictionary [http://www.urbandictionary.com] provides great insights into slang, especially American slang. Definitions are contributed by readers. It used to be a truly great resource to learn more about how people actually spoke in real life. With time, it has lost much of its value. Many entries have turned into jokes more than actual definitions. It is still worth visiting regularly, especially for the most obscure forms of slang.

Ted Duckworth's Dictionary of slang [http://www.peevish.co.uk/slang/] is also well worth visiting. This one focuses on slang used in the U.K. primarily but also covers common American slang.

Google

The Web in English

To get things going, you need to start using the Web in English. We will use Google because it has some pretty smart tools and is ranked the most popular search engine for a number of reasons. Feel free, however, to apply the same tips to any other favorite search engine of your own.

To use Google in English, either click the "Google.com in English" link available at the bottom of the Google homepage, or use this link directly: http://www.google.com/ncr ("NCR" stands for "No Country Redirect"). This will bring you to the American version of Google – totally in English.

Make the above link your homepage. This will get you into the habit of using this page directly to perform your searches. When you want to perform local searches in your native language, you can always resort to your local Google version (link at the bottom of the homepage).

Google NCR is my homepage and I can still go back to my local version of Google (in this example, France) anytime in one click

Picturing it

Translating is a bad habit, because it pushes you to think in your native language, instead of letting ideas and words flow in English directly. A good way to be able to think in English, as indicated in the previous chapter, is to associate pictures (or feelings, or sounds; any sense and mental activity) directly with English words.

One way to build this skill is to link pictures and words directly when you are looking them up. This is especially useful when you have never seen the word before or when the definition in an English-English dictionary may seem a little obscure to you.

As such, when looking a word up, think of looking it up on Google Images. Quite simply, go to Google's image search [http://images.google.com] and search for the word you want to understand.

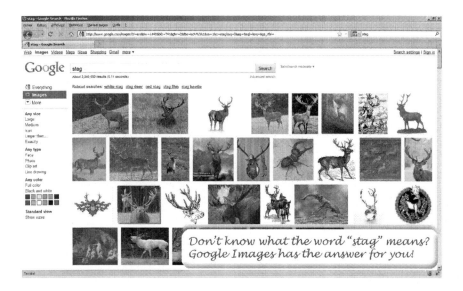

Don't know what the word "stag" means? Google Images has the answer for you!

Concrete examples

For some words, the result will be obvious. You will not even need a dictionary to tell you the meaning, but instead to simply give you the pronunciation.

Try this technique. Search the following words on Google Images: raccoon, heart, ground, goat, Earth, grass, lid, and crowd.

You will also encounter cases where the word may have various different meanings. When that happens, the best thing to do is to search not just for one word, but for a group of words or expression.

Compare searches for: bow, violin bow and ribbon bow; chest, chest tattoos and treasure chest; trunk, elephant trunk, trunk of a car.

Cultural examples

Sometimes, your ability to really understand the word will depend on your own culture. Maybe you do not know the word for that thing in your own native language; one cannot know everything. The point is, you will still be able to *name* that thing, directly in English, the next time you see it.

See for yourself in these examples: hummingbird, power supply, tea ball, scraper, and motherboard.

General words and abstract examples

Sometimes, the result will be not-so-obvious because of the nature of the thing the word is referring to; either because it refers to a quality rather than an object, or, because it refers to something abstract.

Try the following words: glow, answer, lonely, sparkling, and glitter.

The image search still provides value in that it *hints* at what the word means; and, **provides a visual support to help remember the word**. As such, get in the habit of using image searches as a complement, and even sometimes an alternative, to your dictionary.

The majority is right

Google knows what people search for and you can use that fact to learn the most popular way to say something.

This is valuable information because we want to be able to express ourselves just as a native English speaker would. Such a search lets us know how people are actually saying things.

There are two ways to get that information:

Google will suggest corrections

If you search for something (word or expression) that is not the usual form, Google will suggest that you look for the more popular way to say it.

It does not always mean that there is a mistake. For example, if you search for the word "raccoon" (with one 'c'), Google will ask you if you meant "raccoon" (with two 'c'-s). Both spellings are correct, but the second one is the typical spelling.

If you search for "dictionnary"(sic), Google will suggest the correct spelling: "dictionary."

Google lets you check the popularity of a phrase

Let us say you have a doubt regarding a phrase. You are wondering whether or not this is correct. You can run a search for the phrase on Google to see if people actually say that, based on the number of results.

To search for a phrase in Google, simply put it between quotes, like so:

When in doubt, you can also use this technique to compare two phrases, and see which one is more popular and hence more likely to be correct.

Example: Do we say "world of mouth" or "word of mouth"?

From the number of results, we can see that one form is obviously used much more than the other. With over 5 million results, "word of mouth" is indeed the correct expression. With around twenty thousand results, "world of mouth" either contains misspellings or is a play on words.

Overall, this technique lets you estimate if a way to say something is incorrect (no result or hardly any), acceptable (some result) or popular (many results). It is very useful when composing messages.

CONTENT

On the Internet, content is king.

We will talk more about finding information you are passionate about in the next chapter. For now, I would like to show you a couple of well-known content sites and how you can use them to improve your English.

Wikipedia as a translator

Unless you have been living under a rock for the past five years, you must have heard about Wikipedia [http://www.wikipedia.org] by now. Wikipedia: "the free encyclopedia that anyone can edit".

▼ Languages

Български
Català
Česky
Dansk
Deutsch
Español

Русский
Simple English
Suomi
Svenska
ไทย
Türkçe
中文

Maybe you have been using it in your native language until now. What I would like for you to do, however, is to start using it in English. Actually, as you search the Internet in English, you will often encounter Wikipedia entries.

A particular feature that is of interest to us is the "Languages" sidebar. Provided that there exists at least one article in another language for the same subject, the "Language" menu appears on the left and lets you switch to other languages.

For example, this is interesting because if you are on an article written in German or Spanish or Arabic, then you can usually switch to an article on the same subject in English. (Sometimes the other article is a translation; sometimes it is a different article on the same subject, written by different people. It is often a mixture of both.)

Conversely, if you are on an article written in English, you can often swap to an article in your own native language.

What this means is that you can easily read about the same topic in two languages and **this makes figuring out the vocabulary a lot easier**. You can quickly click your way through the English article onto connected subjects or definitions, and switch in-between languages to help you understand everything.

Another benefit is, quite simply, found in the name of the articles. If you are not sure how to say something in English, go to the Wikipedia article on the subject in your native language and, from there, click on the English article link to see how they say it in English. This will not always be a perfect match. At the very least, this gives you a lead on how to talk about the subject in English. For very specific topics that are hard to find in a bilingual dictionary, **this is a great way to know how to say things in English.**

Simple English

Wikipedia also features a language called "Simple English" [http://simple.wikipedia.org]. This is a subset of regular English, with less vocabulary and simpler syntax. This is very useful for someone *just* starting learning and reading English.

VOCABULARY

Surfing the web

A **link** is a clickable piece of text or picture that leads to another page, or to another part of the same page.

A **search engine** is a website whose job is to help you find pages you are interested in, based on the keywords you type.

A **blog** (short for "web log") is a website that usually displays postings in reverse chronological order. They often focus on a specific topic, feature a comments system, and link to similar blogs or websites, making it easy for people to socialize online.

A **browser** is a program used to view web pages, usually available through the Internet or other types of networks.

Wikis are collaborative websites to which readers can easily contribute content.

Google News

Google News [http://news.google.com] makes it easy to read about the news happening anywhere around the world in various languages and with the focus on different countries.

Everybody wants to keep up with the news, but let us be honest, most news is not all that important because it does not directly affect our lives. As such, it makes for great reading material in English (because, if you do not understand each and every thing, it is not the end of the world).

I do not care if you read about sports, show business or more serious topics. As long as you apply yourself to reading in English, you are a winner! Just read what you fancy. You will learn a lot of vocabulary. With the various languages available, you can switch between English and your native language. This makes it easy to compare what you have read in English with what you may read or hear in your own country and language. This is a perfect way to check your understanding and compare languages.

Browse the various English editions available, especially: U.S., UK, Australia, Ireland, Canada and New Zealand.

WRAPPING IT UP

❖ Use the Internet to understand *more quickly*.

❖ Start using English-English dictionaries online to quickly get the *definition* and *hear* the pronunciation.

❖ Get in the habit of looking up words on Google Images to help you *comprehend* and *memorize* the vocabulary more precisely.

❖ Take advantage of the multi-lingual nature of Wikipedia to learn a lot of vocabulary on a specific topic. This can also help you translate more easily when needed.

Chapter 3

Making friends online

English speakers only a click away

"You can make more friends in two months by becoming interested in other people than you can in two years by trying to get other people interested in you."
– Dale Carnegie

The previous two chapters have been the chance to read more English and memorize what you learn more easily, by clarifying and visualizing the meaning of what you see. If you have not practiced those two chapters, please do so now. Reading about what to do is not enough; you need to actually *do it for yourself*.

GOAL & EXIT

Goal

The goal in this chapter is to start expressing yourself in English. Rather than just reading or receiving the information, you will now be *active* and *interact* with other people. The purpose of this chapter is to get you finding your own words to formulate your own ideas.

Exit

Move on to the next chapter once you have made 10 friends on the Internet with whom you can readily chat.

MEETING PEOPLE ONLINE... AND LIKING IT

What you like

The Internet is big enough for you to meet a lot of enjoyable people. One of the best ways to do that is to seek those who share the same interests.

Let us assume your passion in life is film. Then, a good start would be to find a place online where you can discuss your common interest with people just like you. It does not matter from which country you are from, or where they are from (as long as they are native speakers of English). Talking about your passions will make it easier to socialize, easier to provide the required efforts, and it actually may teach you a thing or two (or a hundred) about the things you love. Finding such a place online – where you can discuss your passions – is pretty easy.

This is true about film. This is true about your favorite band, your favorite video game, computer science, musical instruments, sports, travelling...and a thousand other topics. You choose!

Going at your own pace

Starting to express yourself in writing can seem pretty challenging. Luckily, we have options at our disposal to balance the difficulty on this one. Basically, you have two ways to write online:

Self-paced writing

We call self-paced writing any place where you can take as much time as you want to leave a message. Namely, this will mean writing on forums, leaving comments on blogs or writing e-mails.

Real-time writing

We call real-time writing any place where you are supposed to respond instantly, close to the speed of a normal conversation (depending on your typing skills!). Namely, this will include chat rooms, instant messaging applications, and other similar options, such as IRC.

This *is training*

The beauty of both options is that **they leave you enough time to look things up in a dictionary or check on your spelling and grammar before answering.** The first way (self-paced writing) is low-pressure: you have sort of all the time in the world to answer. The second one is more demanding and prepares you to real, in-person conversations.

FINDING YOUR OWN SPOT ON THE NET

Your mission here is simple: find places you like and where you can interact with people on the Internet.

Even if you feel confident with your writing, I suggest you start with *self-paced* writing first. This will give you an opportunity to find your words and shape your own ideas, in English, on topics you like. This will help you write really well, rather than jump into real-time chat, where people write with less care. Once you have gotten in the habit of writing at your own pace, you will move on to real-time chat. Also, this may actually be easier to move from self-paced to real-time because you could then chat with the people you have met on forums, blogs, and similar places.

Where to write

So you need to first find websites you like. This is more of a web search than anything. The best thing to do is to just open Google or your favorite search engine and search for your favorite subject + "blog" or "forum".

For example, if you love Alfred Hitchcock's films, you would search for:

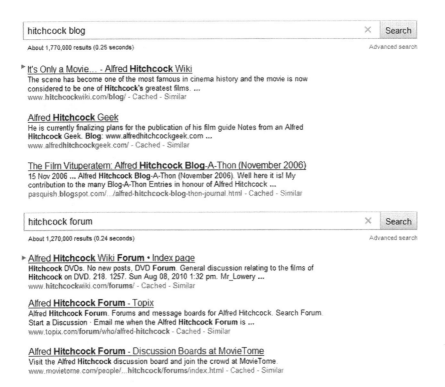

This works especially well for well-defined topics such as: specific hobbies, celebrity's names, or the sciences. For more general terms (such as "movies", "music", "sports") you will get so many results that it can be a hassle to look through them all – or, this could be the chance to check them out and see what the mood is like on each forum, before joining the one you like the best.

If you have a specific topic you would like to discuss, now is your chance to do so. Just look for an online discussion of the subject and get writing. Remember, the more you are interested in the topic, the easier and the more natural it will be for you to participate.

Finding your forum online, as easy as 1-2-3!

❶ Go to Wikipedia, to the version in your own language

Think of your hobby you like the most and locate the Wikipedia article dedicated to it.

❷ Look for the translation in English

In the left column, in the languages area, click the "English" link. This takes you to the English article about your hobby. In the English article, note the name of the article. This is the term you should look for regarding your hobby.

❸ Look for a forum!

On Google or your favorite search engine, look for "forum" and the name of your hobby.

And *voilà!* You should see a list of forums regarding your hobby. Visit 3-5 of them, see which one you like best, and start reading and posting – in English!

What to write

What to write about on a blog is self-evident: you comment on the blog posts that interest you.

On a forum, it is often best to first look for existing topics, rather than create your own.

How to write

Writing is a personal thing that is influenced both by your own personality and your exposure to the subject matter. As such, you will inevitably convey your own personality through your writing. At the same time, you also have to be critical of what you read, to examine what is good English and to decide what you like and do not like. As time goes by, you will be able to express yourself with good English in your own style.

To start with, make profit of the existing posts – be it on a blog or forum – to learn about the vocabulary in use for the topic (a topic you do like, if you chose it properly!). Use the techniques of the previous chapter to make it easier for you to understand what you read.

Next, make sure you know what you want to write about. Here, we are more concerned about *reacting* to what you have just read rather than coming up with new topics. Explore how the post inspired you. How do you feel about what you have just read? What did you particularly like? What does it remind you of? Make a list of all those impressions so as to have a summary of what you want to write about in your post.

It is best to make that list in English obviously, but at this point, it is still acceptable if you do it in your own native language. This is just a list.

Your job is then to expand on each of those points in English. Make a paragraph for each one. If you still feel somewhat insecure about grammar, now is the time to address it. You may also want to use the Google comparison technique shown in the previous chapter, in order to check that what you write is indeed correct English.

Keep in mind that a well-written piece of text is not just about good English construction. It must also be interesting. The two often go hand-in-hand.

As you share your experience and comments, try to bring something valuable. This could be an interesting insight, a funny comment, or information anyone interested in the original post might want to read.

If you need extra help with the vocabulary, use the Wikipedia technique of the previous chapter, and toggle between articles written in English and those in your own language if need be. It is perfectly okay to do your own web-searches and document yourself while writing your message.

Finally, do not try to be perfect. The value of the exercise is in getting into the habit of writing. Of course, your texts in six months will be much better than the ones you write now. As they say: "no worries." Just make sure you post something that you think is valuable, then move on.

The habit of writing

Remember the goal in this chapter is to get you writing frequently. Depending on how much you write and how long it takes you, you should post 1-3 comments a day. If you take the time to write long and detailed replies, this could take you an hour a post. In that case, it is okay to post a reply just once a day. If you go for short replies (1-3 paragraphs), make sure that you write at least three of those per day.

Also, try to be both a friendly and regular visitor, so as to foster a good feeling with the people on the blog or forum. This way, it makes it all very natural to ask for their MSN or Facebook contact in order to chat.

FINDING YOUR WORDS, FASTER

Transitioning

As soon as you feel you can write fast, you should consider moving to real-time chats *in addition* to the forums and blogs mentioned above. You should proceed this way for two main reasons. The first one is to keep working on writing proper English. The other one is to keep networking with people and get more contacts.

Meeting people through the Internet is unlike meeting them in real-life. People may open up more easily because they feel safe, knowing you are miles apart. On the other hand, they can sort of close down because they do not feel safe exchanging contact information with people over the Internet. This is all perfectly okay. Just move on to the next person when you feel someone is not willing to chat with you.

Real-time tools

You have quite a few options to chat with people online. You will find a quick list below, along with a brief overview.

Just use the option most convenient to you and your contact. It is best to send a private message (on forums) or an e-mail (on blogs) to people to exchange contacts and arrange a chat.

Facebook

This is my favorite means of contact nowadays. If you comment on blogs and sign up to be updated on new comments, you will oftentimes receive e-mails from the person running the blog. From there, you may want to look for them on Facebook, based on their e-mail address (just paste the e-mail address in the search field, where you would usually type the person's name) and *voilà*, you can add them to your Facebook contacts.

MSN

MSN used to be like *the* big chat thing in the 2000's. Nowadays, it is still in widespread use but has lost a lot of ground to Facebook. I would usually add people that often post on forums in MSN, because people who are into forums often are into MSN.

Skype

Skype is well-known for its phone-like capabilities. However, you can also use it as a chat system. Not bad if you come across people who use it, since it makes it easy to transition to (quality) voice conversations when you feel like it.

Google Talk

This chat system is compatible with many others but is not used widely. This is handy if you have a Gmail address and your contacts do also because, then you can chat directly from Gmail.

ICQ

ICQ used to be by far the most popular chat client. It never really got the credit or long-term success it deserved. It was eclipsed by Microsoft's MSN and bulldozer-style marketing. There is still a vibrant community around it though.

IRC

IRC is a special case. IRC is not a brand or an instant messaging system like the other systems previously mentioned. You can use IRC to join a lot of different, independent servers. This is great to find chat rooms on highly targeted topics. The added bonus is that people there are often *regulars* and *experts*, who can provide valuable help. Please see the IRC guide in this chapter.

General chat room

If you need a place where you can quickly and easily chat with people, I recommend you try ICQ chat [http://www.icq.com/icqchat/], as you do not need to install anything to use it. This works well as a "Plan-B" when you need to go practice your writing skills live but have no contacts available. Keep in mind that it is better to create some serious contacts, as described above, through blogs/forums (and of course real life!), because then you can have more personal and interesting conversations.

A quick guide to IRC (*Internet Relay Chat*)

On IRC, chat rooms are called "channels".

IRC is especially popular among people who are into technology, video games, and *animes* (animation and comics from Asia, especially Japan). This is sort of the *geeks' chat system*. It easily counts in the tens of thousands of users per server. I recommend it if you are into any of the aforementioned topics.

To use IRC, you will need an IRC client, that is to say: a program to connect to the IRC servers. The most popular one by far is mIRC [http://www.mirc.com], for Windows. Apple users can use Ircle [http://www.ircle.com]. Visit the website and install the program.

Once the program is installed, you will need to choose a nickname and, all especially, an IRC server. If you have no particular ideas, I will introduce you to a couple below:

QuakeNet is great for multiplayer video games. If you love video games, especially computer video games, this is definitely the place to visit. This is also the largest IRC network in the world and is mostly European. Great to hang out and have a laugh.

Freenode is great for new technologies, especially, free software and open-source. A must-visit for any web or software developer. Great to talk shop and get help.

Finally, note that, despite the descriptions above, you can usually find many different topics on each of those IRC servers. As an example, on those networks you can find an *#iphone* channel, even though the main common interest on that network has nothing to do with the iPhone. So once you are on a network, try your luck on subjects you fancy.

VOCABULARY

Language-wise, a major difference between self-paced and real-time discussion is that real-time chat makes heavy use of slang: general slang, Internet slang and acronyms.

To help you figure it all out, here are the main terms in use in chat rooms.

Enjoy using slang in the chat rooms, as this prepares you to talking in person (because of the way real conversations favor brevity). Do keep striving to write perfect English when you participate in forums and on blogs, forever. This is important to have both skills: the ability to write great English; and, the ability to talk in a more relaxed, casual, way.

WRAPPING IT UP

❖ Find blogs or forums on your favorite topics.

❖ Participate in those websites regularly so people remember you and you remember them.

❖ Get in touch with the people you appreciate, in order to chat with them in real-time.

❖ Keep at it until you have at least 10 friends you can regularly chat with.

Online slang and acronyms

AFAIK	As Far As I Know
AFK	Away From Keyboard
ASAP	As Soon As Possible
ASL	Age, Sex, Location
ATM	At The Moment
BBL	Be Back Later
BBIAB	Be Back In A Bit
B/C	Because
BRB	Be Right Back ("I will be right back")
BS	B*llsh*t
BTW	By The Way
CU or Cya	See You ("See you later")
FYI	For Your Information
G2G or GTG	Gotta Go ("I have (got) to go")
IDK	I Don't Know
IRL	In Real Life
J/K	Just Kidding
K	O.K.
L8R or LTR	Later ("See you later")
LMAO	Laughing My Ass Off (Laughing a lot)
LOL	Laughing Out Loud or Lots of Laughter
NVM	Never mind
NP	No problem
OMG	Oh My God!
PLS or PLZ	Please
PPL	People
ROFL	Rolling On The Floor Laughing
THX	Thanks
WB	Welcome Back
WTF	What The F***
YW	You're welcome

Chapter 4

Virtual Worlds

Practice makes perfect

"To know and not to do is not yet to know."
– Zen Wisdom

GOAL & EXIT

Goal

The goal in this chapter is to develop your ability to *learn visually*, to *interact* in a virtual world and to *chat* with other people – all at the same time. This will help you build strong foundations for simultaneously *understanding* and *expressing* yourself. It is also an opportunity to gain a lot of vocabulary.

Exit

Keep at this activity for two weeks, about an hour a day. If you like video games, keep at it later on. If you do not like video games and virtual worlds so much, move on, but do try to keep what you have learned about learning visually and having people explain things to you in English.

VIDEO GAMES... REALLY?

Traveling from home

The world speaks more and more English. However, finding people to practice with is not always an easy task.

Without traveling, what can you do to get all those little details that make you feel you are abroad?!

You would need to travel to learn English; but you need to learn English to feel comfortable traveling. The way out of this vicious circle is to use a new, efficient, underestimated – yet full of promise medium – virtual worlds and video games.

This is a great way to start seeing, reading, listening to, choosing, thinking, acting and chatting in English.

Play along and you will have an excellent means to learn a lot of English quickly, easily and effortlessly. You know how airplane pilots use flight simulators to train? Well, this chapter is about having your own personal English simulator.

Virtual worlds or video games?

Definitions

Let us first define the difference between virtual worlds and video games. The difference may not be familiar to everyone.

Virtual worlds will be any world on a computer or video game console that lets you navigate in it, interact with what you find, as well as interact with other people along the way. They do not necessarily have a definite purpose, except to socialize online and have fun. For our purposes, we will be using Second Life, an online world where people can do pretty much anything, including: buy land, build houses, create clothes, fly, and, of course chit-chat with one another.

Video games will be any game played on a computer or a video game console. Oftentimes, video games will be virtual worlds as well. I draw a distinction. Virtual worlds typically let you wander freely within them, with no specific purpose except socializing. Video games *will* have a defined purpose. You will have a mission to fulfill and rules to follow.

So to sum it up:

Virtual worlds: you go around freely within the world, to have fun and meet people online.

Video games: you have objectives to fulfill (e.g., quests, with levels to complete and puzzles to solve).

Purpose

We will deal with virtual worlds, mostly with Second Life in particular, because this is a big, highly popular world that is heavily populated, and free-of-charge. You will be meeting people within a couple of minutes of installing the software.

We will be using video games especially for people who like them. If you are not into video games that is fair enough; you can skip this part and move on. However, if you do like (love?!) video games, you will be using them in a new and very clever way.

SECOND LIFE

Overview

Second Life is a huge, online, 3D world, where people can chat, interact, dress up, build houses... Pretty much anything you can do in the real world – hence the name. It has been around since 2003 and seems to be here to stay.

Even though this is "just" a 3D world, it is a pretty special one. It features its own economy. People can own land there;

people can create interactive 3D objects and sell them. It has been used for real-life events, such as online courses from renowned universities and concerts from famous bands. It has been used for experiments in both business and sociology. It counts a number of companies with virtual offices in it, as well as some embassies.

This is quite a one-of-a-kind 3D world and is almost as diverse as our "first" real world and real-life.

Getting started

Installing

Choose a new name, create your own look, and join millions of people online! Just go to this address to download the software and join the fun:

http://secondlife.com/join

Simply create an account there and follow the instructions. Much of it is automatic. Last time I tried, on an old PC with a normal broadband connection, this only took a couple of minutes.

Warning!

Due to its exceptional levels of freedom, the standard version of Second Life is for adults only.

People under 18 should use Teen Second Life, which is for people under 18 exclusively. It is located here:

http://teen.secondlife.com

First steps

The world of Second Life regularly evolves. When you first join, you will be in a place that gives you some help on how to move and use Second Life.

You should learn the four basic moves: moving around (arrow keys), zooming in ('alt' key + click + mouse), flying ('page-up' key), and interacting (right-click).

From there, you will soon be able to teleport to a different place in the virtual world, such as places to explore or places where to meet people.

You should also learn to use the interface, which is rather self-explanatory. Learn to review the chat history (click on the button next to the chat input box) and to teleport ("World" menu).

What's next?

In the end, Second Life is a 3D chat. Just walk around and chat with people. The chance you have is that, contrary to traditional chat-rooms, you have the chance to have the world around you provide topics of conversations.

For example:

- Ask people which places they recommend you visit.
- Talk to them about their outfits.
- Join the conversations.
- Make fun and comments about what you see and hear.

Basically, just have a good time practicing your English.

Finally, the more you invest yourself in this, the more reward you will reap.

It is okay to just use this as a tool, to chit-chat with strangers once in a while.

However, as you spend more time in it, you will feel more comfortable using it and will know the nicer places to hang out. In itself, this will bring more topics of conversation and you will speak with more and more people.

You are on your own for the rest of your exploration of Second Life. Just keep to the schedule: one hour a day for two weeks; at least 3-5 days a week.

VIDEO GAMES

Overview

The great thing about video games is that you are in charge of what is happening on screen. There is a whole world of difference between being passive and being active. Try and remember something you have learned to do: do you learn better when people show you and do it for you; or, do you learn better when people explain to you and let you try it yourself? Being in charge and in control is what makes video games such a great way to learn and makes them valuable products full of educational promise.

These days, video games are meeting with more and more success, appealing to a wider audience and maturing as a medium. At the same time, they are meeting with a lot of bad press, facing a lot of criticism, because of violent content and, also maybe because of their appeal to the youth, something which does not usually please parents and educators. The truth remains that video games are now available in a wide variety of genres, in a way very similar to how there are films available for all tastes. If video games are not your cup of tea, I can only ask you to keep an open mind and see how you could use them to expand your vocabulary and practice your English. We will do something similar in a later chapter about TV and movies.

The great thing about learning English using video games is that instead of just seeing or reading *the word,* **you see and use** *the object* referring to the word. This is similar to what we have seen about learning visually except this is much more interactive and as such, you gain an experience of the words you use, making them much easier to remember. It is like traveling abroad, except much easier, much more flexible and cheaper to do on a daily basis!

What we will see next is how different genres of video games will help you practice various English skills. I am not covering all genres because, even though some of them may be a lot of fun, they do not necessarily have a lot to do with language skills (e.g., Tetris!).

Your job is to pick at least one game, order it in its English version and play it from beginning to end. In doing so, you will learn a lot without much effort.

Buyers' guide

Picking a video game to help your English

Here is an overview of the different genres available and how they can help you practice your English.

<u>Role-Playing Games (RPGs)</u>

Role-playing games (RPGs) are games where the player assumes the role of one or more characters, in order to participate in countless adventures. Those games usually focus on story-telling, character development, and a high degree of liberty.

For example, you will create a character and choose his name and attributes (intelligence, charisma, strength, speed…), his specialty or profession (a thief? a warrior? a wizard?) and will then set yourself on a major quest (saving the world?), while completing various miscellaneous tasks (killing a dragon, saving a village).

This genre is often, but not exclusively set in an heroic-fantasy setting (think "Lord of the Rings").

These games are a great way to learn *a whole lot* of vocabulary. You usually find a complete virtual world in them, with lots of things to do (as opposed to Second Life, where you find a vast world but in which you are mostly there to chat – not do things). For example, in an RPG, you could go into a shop and buy various items: as you do so, usually, you simply have to let the mouse cursor wander on top of an item for the name to be displayed. It is a quick and easy way to learn the name of many objects. As you use those later on during the game, you will be reminded of their name and memorize them better. You do not just learn vocabulary; you also learn to use it since these games usually also feature a huge amount of interactive dialogue, which makes them great for practicing your reading skills.

This genre is at the crossroad of many art forms, with a mix of visual arts, story-telling, dialogue, and music. It is like the interactive version of a mixture of novels and movies. For all these reasons, it comes as the #1 recommendation on this list.

Major titles:

- Fable series (2004–present)
- Fallout series (1997–present)
- The Elder Scrolls series (1992–present)
- Final Fantasy series (1987–present)

Simulation games

In simulation (or "sim") games, you are in charge of managing a specific task that could apply to real-life. In one of those, for example, Capitalism, you have to build a company from the ground up – buying resources and transforming them into products.

Those games are great for learning a large, diverse vocabulary. Playing "The Sims" in English will teach you all the typical words you need to know around the house, for example.

You can also find more technical simulation games, such as flight simulators or realistic race simulators.

Major titles:

- The Sims series (2000–present)
- Capitaslim series (1995–2001)
- Civilization series (1991–present)
- SimCity series (1989–present)

First-person shooters (FPS)

First-person shooters are among the most violent video

games: you run around with guns and have to shoot your opponent. They do have bad press because of the violence, so remember one thing: this is just a virtual game. ☺ This is also a great way to relax, sort of like a stress-ball-version of a video game.

What will be of interest to us is playing them online. The people who are really into those games tend to organize themselves into communities – running websites, forums, and competitions. Playing these games offline can be a lot of fun and will teach you some vocabulary (especially around weapons!)... However, they will prove really useful for your English once you start playing them online, for this is the chance to join players from dozens of different countries and practice your English.

Major titles:

- Call of Duty series (2003–present)
- Counter-Strike (1999–present)
- Halo series (2001–present)
- Unreal Tournament series (1999–present)
- Quake series (1996–present)

Online Role-Playing Games

In addition to the traditional computer or console role-playing games mentioned previously, you will also find online role-playing games, often called "Massively Multiplayer Online Role-Playing Games" or "MMORPG".

The story line is usually much weaker than that of an offline RPG and the game may not always look as pretty or detailed. What those games lose in depth or richness, however, they gain in inter-activity. Similar to the way first-person shooters are played online, people who are into those games are usually very well organized and form a real online community.

Virtual Worlds

Those are good reasons to practice your vocabulary and meet other players online.

Major titles:

- A i o n (2008–present)
- The Lord of the Rings Online (2007–present)
- Guild Wars (2005–present)
- City of Heroes (2004–present)
- World of Warcraft (2004–present)

Other genres

All games do not fit nicely into the categories aforementioned. Many being a mix of genres. As such, most games borrowing elements from RPG games or with a rich story line make for good games to learn vocabulary. Typically, the more visual and interactive the game, and the more freedom in it, the better for your English.

Major titles:

- Assassin's Creed series (2007–present)
- Grand Theft Auto (GTA) series (2001–present)
- Mafia series (2002–present)

Where to buy

Oftentimes, the local version of a game contains the English version also. However, that is *not always* the case. Check the games box in store.

If in doubt, buy the game abroad, online. You can find it on sites like Amazon.com for example.

For console games, be careful, because some games may only be played on consoles from a certain region. This is known as "regional lockout". Verify that the game can be played in your country before you buy.

WRAPPING IT UP

❖ Sign up to Second Life and join the virtual world at least three days a week, for two weeks, an hour each day.

❖ Find and play a video game you like, in English.

❖ Use the visual and interactive nature of those medium to learn and *use what you learn* (by clicking on it; by talking about it). The goal is to expand your vocabulary.

❖ Focus on having a good time and, in the virtual worlds, on socializing. As you do so, you will learn a lot without much effort.

Chapter 5

Accent Training

Train your ears, train your tongue

"The quantity of consonants in the English language is constant. If omitted in one place, they turn up in another. When a Bostonian 'pahks his cah', the lost r's migrate southwest, causing a Texan to 'warsh his car' and 'invest in erl wells.'"
– Anonymous

GOAL & EXIT

Goal

The purpose of this chapter is for you to know and hear all of the English sounds, pronounce them properly, and lose your accent.

Exit

Move on to the next chapter once you know the English sounds, which means knowing the list of English sounds and being able to produce them. By doing so, you should also be in the process of reducing your accent.

HEARING AND PRONOUNCING PROPERLY

We only produce the sounds we hear or think we hear. As such, it is critical to *hear properly* in order to *pronounce properly*.

Ear training

A common mistake when trying to pronounce an English or foreign word is to try and adapt the sound to our native language, as if something was "bad" with the foreign sound. This is a natural process, due to the fact that we have been trained our whole life to only hear certain sounds in speech.

From using our own native language, **we have grown used to hearing** *only* **specific sounds**. As such, when we hear something that is different from what we know, we assume unconsciously that there is something wrong with it, that there is a mistake.

This is as if we had a list or map in our heads of all the sounds that are acceptable. When we hear new, foreign sounds and they do not match the list or map, something strange occurs. We do not accept them at first.

However, to speak English properly, you need to update that list or map, to take into account *new* sounds. Some of the English sounds may be similar to sounds found in your native language... but even then, they are still different and you need to hear those distinctions in order to pronounce them slightly differently. Some of those sounds may be completely unlike any sound you have in your native language... When that happens, it will be easier to distinguish them but it will also take a little more effort to clearly hear them and to precisely produce them. Finally, a few of those sounds may be identical; however, the fact that they are surrounded by sounds that are not identical means we will have to learn using them in combination with new, different sounds.

To get used to the English sounds, you will need to *unlearn* a little. You will need to stop treating English sounds as "bad sounds." You will need to accept the differences in order to hear them properly. Some of this happens on a conscious level, by paying attention; some of this happens on an unconscious level – through repeated exposure to the English language.

In doing so, your brain will end up accepting those sounds, until they become part of your mental lexicon of existing sounds. This is also why daily practice is required: the more you are exposed to the (at first) *unusual* sounds of English, the easier it will be to accept them as natural, normal, and correct sounds.

This is also why it is easier to learn a third or fourth language than it is to learn a second language... By the third or fourth language, we have already been through the process of getting out of our habits in order to hear new sounds.

The good news is that this list of new sounds is limited. Once you know them, your job is almost over and you can start speaking English near perfection! You will have developed the ability to recognize each of the English sounds.

Ear-training is all about developing the brain's ability to perceive new sounds. This is a process of opening up.

"Tongue training"

In a similar fashion, we are also used to only producing (*i.e.*, pronouncing) very specific sounds – those found in our native language. We assume various mouth, tongue and vocal system positions to do just that. As such, our vocal system is trained to being *only* in certain specific positions. **Speaking English properly will mean learning *new* positions for the vocal system.**

I like to call this process "tongue-training," to reflect the muscular nature of the action. We could call that "accent training" but this term is vague. More accurately, we could call it "pronunciation training," but this fails to recognize a simple truth: pronouncing the right sound, in a foreign language like

English, depends heavily on *muscle* activity. You need to learn to position your tongue with precision, in new ways, in order to produce chiefly English sounds.

To sum it up: producing new sounds means placing your vocal system in new configurations. This is the process of controlling your mouth and tongue muscles.

Do the following exercise to bring this simple fact to conscious awareness. Alone in a quiet room, read the following text and do what is written in it at the same time:

"Try, out loud, to speak with a *deep voice*... then *through your nose*... Try to speak with your mouth *wide open*... then with your mouth *in a round shape*... Try to pronounce long vowels, like "*ooooo*"... then short vowels, like "*o*"; do the same with other vowels... Try to speak the "*s*" sound under several variations... "*sssss*"... "*zzzzz*"... "*th*"... You have quite a few different ways to pronounce things."

Do the exercise once more and, this time try to locate *where* the difference in sound comes from. What is the difference, in your mouth, in-between two sounds? What is the tongue position?

Here are some more questions to make it clear that you have options as to how to make sounds:

- What do you do differently in your mouth when you say "*o*" and "*a*"?

- What do you do differently when you say "*sss*", "*zzz*" and "*th*..." ?

- What do you do differently when you say "*b*" and "*p*"? Or when you say "*t*" and "*d*"?

- What do you do differently when you say a long "*o*" vs. a short "*o*"? A long "*i*" vs. a short "*i*"?

Feel the difference in how you position your mouth and tongue.

From now on, whenever you hear an English sound that does not sound familiar, try to hear it properly and then try to pronounce it. *Feel* where your tongue is located in your mouth at that very moment; and how the rest of the vocal system is positioned.

You can also do that as you practice chapter one, with songs; or as you practice other chapters, especially the chapter on TV, and the one on audio books.

Phonetics

What we have seen above is known as phonetics – without the technical terms and details.

Phonetics is the study of sounds in the human speech, especially at it applies to a specific language, including ways to represent those sounds in written form.

The value of phonetics is that it will clarify what we have just discussed. Instead of just talking about how the tongue can be positioned in various ways, you will find charts that show you *where* the tongue is to be positioned, for each specific English sound.

USING PHONETICS

As we have seen above, two things are critical: hearing the sounds (this means opening and training your ears, or rather, *brains*) and producing the sounds (this means positioning the tongue and the rest of the vocal system properly).

The study of English phonetics is the study of all sounds that are chiefly found in English.

All English sounds

English sounds can be divided into three categories: consonants; vowels, and diphthongs/triphthongs. We will review what each of those is and in so doing, we will see *all* of the sounds found in the English language.

This section can and should be used later on for reference purposes. Come back and check it again later, as you make progress through this book, especially when you reach the chapters that work on your spoken English (TV, audio books, and meeting people). By the end of this chapter, you will know exactly what *each* of the English sounds is and you will be able to hear and pronounce them correctly.

To understand these sounds better, it is best to have audio files available. I suggest going to an online dictionary to look up each example word given here. This way, you just have to click on the pronunciation icon in the dictionary to actually hear the word, instead of guessing how it is pronounced. For this, TheFreeDictionary [http://www.thefreedictionary.com] is really good. It will show you the spelling of the word, its standard phonetics notation in IPA and give you audio files to listen to both in American English and British English.

Finally, it is also a good idea to open up your own bilingual dictionary – if you have one – as those usually compare phonetics between English and your native language. Check the phonetics page, usually found at the start of the dictionary. This way, you will be able to compare consonants and vowels found in *your* native tongue and those found in English. Some will be identical; some will not.

A word on IPA

IPA stands for the International Phonetics Alphabet. It provides a standardized way to write out the pronunciation of a word, regardless of the language.

In most languages, including English, letters are not pronounced the same way everywhere. The pronunciation varies depending on the surrounding letters or the position of a syllable in the word. In IPA notation, however, each IPA letter matches one sound – and one sound only.

It is a great way to compare languages.

(Some dictionaries, however, do not use the IPA and, instead, use their own systems to represent the pronunciation. This is the case at Answers.com for example).

Let us now review all of the English sounds! See the tables below and **listen to each of the example words** in your online dictionary to know what they *really* sound like.

Consonants

A consonant is a speech sound produced by partial or complete closure of the air stream.

Literally, consonant means "with sound."

Consonant	Examples
b	but, lab, about
d	dog, bed, adapt
ʤ	joy, rage, enjoy
f	fire, life, after
g	go, egg, forget
h	hot, hat, hand
j	you, yes, onion
k	cat, track, backpack
l	love, all
m	me, him, amazing
n	no, know, on, thin
ŋ	sing, bank, think
p	pen, top, empty
ɹ	run, bar, arrive
s	song, bus, ice
ʃ	shine, fish, ashore
t	team, pet, entrance
tʃ	chat, search, nature
θ	thing, path, a breath
ð	that, mother, to breathe
v	victory, live, vivid
w	we, with, away
z	zoom, buzz, business, easy
ʒ	pleasure, vision, garage, beige

Notes:

- All of those sounds exist in the various English accents.
- Please note that "*no*" and "*know*" sound exactly the same. The letter 'k' in "know" and other words starting in "kn-" are silent.
- The letter and sound '*h*' *is* pronounced in words starting with 'h'. This is the same sound as a sigh.

- To make things easier, many books write the 'ɹ' consonant (a reversed 'r') as a regular 'r'. Technically, however, in IPA, 'ɹ' and 'r' are not the same sounds; the 'ɹ' sound found in English sounds a little like 'w'.

Vowels

A vowel is a speech sound produced by letting the air flow through the oral cavity.

The word comes from a Latin word meaning "voice."

Vowel	Examples
ɑː *-or-* ɒ	car, ask, hot, shot
ʌ	plus, love, sun, son
ɔː	all, short, thought, draw
uː	fool, food, dude
ʊ	full, foot, wood, would
ɜ	learn, curve, bird
ə	about, alone, system
ɪ	bit, fit, pitch, live
æ	bad, hat, cat
ɛ *-or-* e	bed, head, said
iː	beat, feet, peach, leave

Notes:

- Either 'ɑː' or 'ɒ' is used, depending on the accent. 'ɑː' is an unrounded vowel, this means that the mouth is *not* rounded when the sound is pronounced. This is typically how an American would pronounce "car, ask, hot, shot" and how a British person would pronounce "car, ask". On the contrary, 'ɒ' *is* a rounded vowel; this means the mouth (the lips) *is* rounded when the sound is pronounced. This is how a British person would pronounce "hot, what, shot". Actually, a quick trick to mimic a British accent is to round your mouth as you speak – try it! More on accents later in this chapter.

- 'ʌ' sound: "sun" and "son" sound exactly the same.
- 'ʊ' sound: "wood" and "would" sound exactly the same.
- 'ə' sound: is a mid-central vowel; the sound originates from the center of the mouth and is hardly pronounced at all. It is a sound very common in the English language. "about, alone, system" is almost pronounced "'bout, 'lone, syst'm". This vowel is, technically, called the "schwa" and is something of a silent 'e.'
- 'ɑː', 'ɔː', 'uː' and 'iː' are long vowels and will necessarily sound longer than the short vowels. You do not need to overdo it but you do need to get used to it. This is especially important for the 'iː' sound as the length of the vowel carries meaning: "leave" is not the same as "live", for example, and in speech, only the length of the vowel lets us know the difference between the two words. Same thing for "pitch" and "peach". Rather than making the long vowel really extra-long, think that short vowels are pretty short and may well be shorter than vowels in your own native language. Compare the short and long vowels in English by listening to audio files; also compare the length of those vowels to similar vowels in your native language.
- Either 'ɛ' or 'e' is used, depending on the accent. For 'ɛ', the tongue is positioned slightly lower than for 'e.' This is what an American would typically use, whereas a British speaker would use the other form. (More on tongue position later in this chapter.)

Diphthongs

A diphthong is a speech sound that begins as one vowel sound and turns into another vowel within the same syllable.

This is also called a "gliding vowel," which refers to the fact this is a shift (a glide) from one vowel into another.

The word comes from Greek and means "double sound."

Diphthong	Examples
ɔɪ	boy, toy, enjoy
oʊ -*or*- əʊ	no, flow, row, go
ʊə	sure, poor, tour
ɪə	peer, near, here
aɪ	eye, I, hi, my, pie
aʊ	house, cow, now
eə	there, their, bare, bear, hair
eɪ	pay, pain, ray, rain, raise

Notes:

- Given their composite nature, it is easiest to pronounce these once you can pronounce the standard vowels.
- Please note that some of the vowel sounds composing those diphthongs are only found in diphthongs and triphthongs; they are not used on their own as "pure" or single vowel sounds. This is the case for 'o' and 'a.'
- **To practice diphthongs:** practice pronouncing the starting vowel in the diphthong; then practice pronouncing the ending vowel in the diphthong; then practice the diphthong itself, by shifting from one sound to the other.
- Please note that "eye" and "I" sound exactly the same; same for "there" and "their" and "bare" and "bear."
- Either 'oʊ' or 'əʊ' is used, depending on the accent, just like we have seen for the vowels. The 'oʊ' sound would be used in American English; 'əʊ' would be used in British English.

Triphthongs

Similarly to diphthongs, produced as glides between two vowels, the English language also features triphthongs, which are a glide between *three* successive vowels, within the same syllable.

Literally, triphthong means "three sounds."

Triphthong	Examples
ɔɪə	employer, loyal, royal
oʊə -*or*- əʊə	slower, lower, mower
aʊə	shower, power, hour
aɪə	fire, liar, buyer
eɪə	player, payer, layer

Notes:

- Those sound pretty much like several of the diphthongs we have just seen, except we add one last glide toward the mid-central vowel 'ə' (the "schwa", something of a silent 'e').

Making it all seem natural

I realize that this is a lot of ground to cover in one session. Before we proceed with the rest of this chapter, please take the time to review these four lists again. Take time to **listen to the samples in an online dictionary and to repeat them.**

Take the time to feel how you position your mouth, tongue, and vocal system as you try to reproduce the sounds you hear. I have not given you many details yet – this is so as to push you to really listen and pay attention as you try hearing and repeating those sounds. Treat it as a game and play along!

Also realize that there are only really three things to master: being able to hear and pronounce *consonants* (usually the easier parts – as most are common to many languages), being able to hear and pronounce the *vowels*, and being able to *compose* vowels into diphthongs or triphthongs.

In the next section, we will talk about vowels in more detail, to make it easier for you to *precisely* locate and position them in your mouth. This will make *producing* the sounds much easier.

Vowels in pictures

Pronouncing vowels properly is the key to speaking good, easy-to-understand English.

Recall what I mentioned at the beginning of this chapter about "tongue training". The ability to produce English vowels correctly comes from the ability to correctly place the tongue at the exact location.

As such, pronunciation does not only have to do with hearing and repeating. It also has to do with *muscle memory*: once you remember how to place your tongue and/or lips to produce a specific sound, the job is done.

At first, getting the positions right will require conscious effort. With practice, this will become a new habit and pronouncing English properly will be automatic. (This will be strengthened and made effortless by the chapters on TV and audio books.)

Introducing phonetic charts

Phonetics makes use of very helpful diagrams that outline the difference between all existing vowels. Simply put, a vowel sound can either come from far into the mouth or from close to the teeth (this is the horizontal axis). A vowel can also come from close to the bottom of the mouth or from close to the roof of the mouth (this is the vertical axis). **This refers to the position of the tongue in your mouth when you pronounce the vowel.**

Here is a diagram of the mouth at rest:

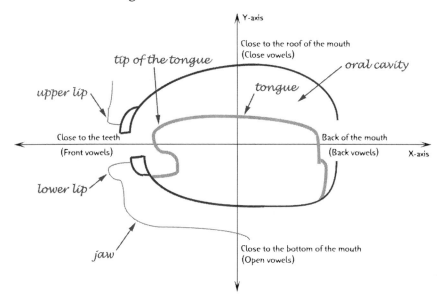

Now, here is a diagram of the mouth again, when pronouncing the vowel 'iː' and another one for the vowel 'ʌ.' Please note the position of the tip of the tongue:

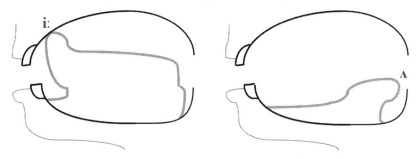

Try pronouncing those two vowels, for example 'iː' as in "**feet**" and 'ʌ' as in "**plus**". See how, indeed, one vowel is located close to the roof of the mouth and toward the front teeth ('**i**:'). The other vowel is located toward the bottom and back of the mouth ('ʌ'). You now have a way, with such diagrams, to position those vowels in your own mouth and get the positions right.

Now, we can position all English vowels the same way on a diagram and thus understand where they are formed. The combined diagram looks like this:

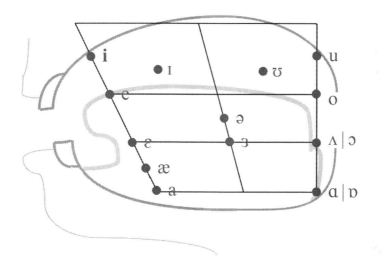

The position of the vowel is the position of the *tip of your tongue* when pronouncing the vowel. As such, what makes the difference between two vowels is where you position the tongue. You need to train your muscles to know exactly where to position the tongue to produce the right vowel.

Note: by convention, when you have two vowels at the same spot, the first one is unrounded (meaning the lips are relaxed), while the second one is rounded (meaning the mouth and lips form a circular opening).

Such a diagram is called an "IPA vowels chart".

Are you thinking this is a lot of vowels right now? Well this is quite alright. I have included all vowels from the two major English accents on this chart. When you take a chart for one specific accent, as we will do soon, the chart is lighter and easier to read.

What I would like you to do now is check the vowels, diphthongs, and triphthongs lists again and this time: **use the last diagram** to help you physically locate the vowels, in your mouth. *You need to feel it and get the positions right.*

TIPS AND TRICKS

Besides the theory and charts behind phonetics, a number of tips and tricks will help you in mastering your spoken English.

Use slang

People do not speak the way they write. Some syllables and even complete words are forgotten when speaking.

The simplest example of this is contractions, which are frequent enough, actually, to be found in written form. "can't" and "cannot" mean the same thing. Yet, "cannot" and "can not" are the proper written forms. In speech, people will usually say "can't."

Another example of contraction would be people saying "you're" instead of "you are" or "c'mon" instead of "come on" or "let's" instead of "let us."

See just how it is in your own native language. Be it SMS messages, Internet chat, or just good old regular speech, people tend to altogether *skip* the syllables that are hardly heard.

Basically, if you can *make a word shorter* and people still understand you, then it will tend to happen. This is quite natural. People like to talk fast and not waste time.

Rap music

Good examples of this can be found in rap music. If you like rap, go back and practice chapter 1 again – this time, with a rap song. You will see many examples of slang and in doing so, discover great examples of how one can shorten words while still retaining their meaning.

Adverbs

Adverbs tend to be shortened to actually look like adjectives. For example, when someone says "Come here! Quick!" he actually means "Come here! Quickly!". Shortening adverbs ("quickly") into adjectives ("quick") does not prevent people from understanding, so this phenomenon tends to happen often.

This does not mean you should shorten everything but it does mean you should be aware that it does happen.

Common speech

As you gain more experience with English as a spoken language, you will notice that some words disappear altogether in speech, especially in familiar talk, but reappear in formal talk and in writing.

This is great information because this means that those words will be spoken more softly in formal talk. This gives you clues as to which words carry a lot of weight and which ones you do *not* need to stress.

For example, people will often say "How you doing?" instead of "How are you doing?"

Keep observing such things and you will be soon able to add good rhythm to the way you speak. This will make your words flow in a more real and natural way.

Sight

As you listen to people talk, be it in person, on TV, or in the movies, observe the way their lips and mouth move; as if reading their lips.

This is good practice because this will train your muscle memory as it relates to speech.

Observe which muscles are moving the speed at which each part moves... Try to reproduce parts of what you have heard, along with the muscle movements you have observed. This will train you to reproduce real and accurate English sounds. This is something rather intuitive but do try it.

Congratulations!

You now have a strong basis in English phonetics. In and of itself, this is enough **to help you speak better English than most people in your native country**. Phonetics is highly underestimated and yet is one of the main keys to speaking great English.

Try and check again this section later as you proceed with the rest of the book (especially TV, audio books and meeting people). The goal is for you to easily hear and pronounce each and every English consonant, vowel, diphthong and triphthong.

In the next section, we will have a look at the various English accents and help you pick one you like.

ENGLISH ACCENTS

Why do people have an accent?

Have you ever met someone who still could not get rid of his foreign accent, even after years of living in a new country? The reasons for this can be many but here are a few pointers:

- A desire to show where you are from.
- Being afraid of looking silly when/if attempting the local accent.
- While speaking: trying to "read words in one's mind" instead of speaking directly.
- While reading: not knowing the proper way each word is pronounced.

- A lack of observation as to how words are pronounced when talking (same point as above but applied to meeting people).
- Lack of training in *listening* to the sounds of the language.
- Lack of training in *producing* the sounds of the language.
- Lack of motivation; lack of desire to change or learn.

I would like you to take a moment to reflect on the reasons above. See how some of those could maybe (just maybe!), apply to you. Please take about 10 minutes to do so.

Done? OK. Great! Oftentimes, realizing you do one of those things is enough to get rid of it.

Now, you also may realize that there is a great advantage in speaking with as little a foreign accent as possible. Not only will people understand you more easily, but they will also tend to take you more seriously. Add to that the pleasure of knowing that what you say sounds truly *English* when you are speaking – which helps boost self-confidence!

What is in an accent?

So what then is an accent? An accent is a set of phonetics habits, which are usually found common to a group.

This simply means that from one region to the other, or from one group of people to another – even though they all speak English – there will be slight differences in the way they pronounce the language.

The charts we have seen make it easy to list the differences: we just list the sounds used within *one* accent. There can be differences in the way consonants are pronounced (especially when English is spoken by non native speakers – especially if they have never learned about phonetics) but most differences are about the vowels.

One could also go one step further and say that everyone has his own accent. Two persons with the same social and regional background can indeed pronounce English slightly differently... Simply put, the differences are usually less numerous and more subtle in that case.

Checking one's accent

How can you tell where someone is from? Well, you can simply ask them out of curiosity. This often makes for interesting conversations since there are so many accents in English – even within one and the same country.

In the case of media celebrities, simply look them up online. Try to know where the person was born and raised. Wikipedia and IMDb [http://www.imdb.com] work great for this.

The best way to acquire an accent remains to try and imitate it – exposure to the language plays a big part here. We will have a look at two major accents and an overview of the main accents in use throughout the world.

Show me the accents!

General American (GA) and Received Pronunciation (RP)

General American (GA) can be considered the standard accent in the United States. It refers to the most neutral and most easily understandable accent in the U.S. This is typically the accent heard on the radio and on the news (also called "Network English"). This is also the accent of people living in the midwestern United States.

Received Pronunciation (RP) can be considered the standard accent in the United Kingdom. This has long been considered the way English is "supposed" to be spoken. It is rather prestigious and closely associated with the upper class. It has long been the only accent heard on the BBC. It is also called "Queen's English," "King's English" or "BBC English."

Here are the IPA vowel charts for each accent:

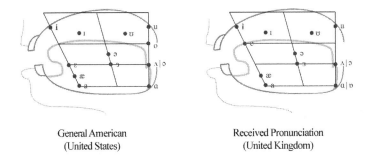

General American
(United States)

Received Pronunciation
(United Kingdom)

Try and compare them. Try and pronounce each of the vowels with example words. This will give you an idea of the differences and similarities between the two accents.

Note on consonants: there *is* a difference between General American and Received Pronunciation regarding consonants. In General American, the 'r' (or, rather, 'ɹ' in IPA) is always pronounced. In Received Pronunciation, it is usually only pronounced if there is a vowel after it. When the 'r' is pronounced, this is called a rhotic accent (as in GA); when the 'r' is not pronounced, this is called a non-rhotic accent (as in RP).

Comparing British and American pronunciations

Cambridge has a quality online dictionary for listening to the pronunciation in either RP or GA and see the IPA transcriptions for each accent:

http://dictionary.cambridge.org

The interface could be better but the features are great.

Overview of other English accents

There are many different English accents and a description of those could fill several books in its own right. What I would like to do here is give you an overview of the main English accents, so that you know they exist and are not surprised when you encounter them.

Australian English (AuE)

Many vowels are pronounced closer to the mouth roof. Most diphthongs are pronounced differently from British and American accents. It sounds similar to Received Pronunciation, yet, the higher vowels and different diphthongs are enough to create a discernible difference.

Canadian English (CaE)

Most of the vowel sounds usually found near the front of the mouth are pronounced lower (closer to the bottom of the mouth) than in RP or GA. Moreover, diphthongs are pronounced higher before certain consonants. The overall feel is that of a deep yet changing voice, with variations between lower vowels and high vowels.

New York accent

This is a high-pitched and very nasal accent. This is a non-rhotic accent, like Received Pronunciation is, meaning the 'r' are not pronounced at the end of syllables. (See the quote at the beginning of this chapter!)

Southern American English (SAE)

The accent varies from region to region. Overall, this is a slow accent with its own kind of sing-song sounds built into the pronunciation. A particular fact is that some vowels actually turn into diphthongs. Additionally, some 's' sounds turn into 'd' sounds.

African American Vernacular English (AAVE)

The accent is rather uniform throughout the USA. It is overall a smooth accent, with the larynx not vibrating on certain consonants and diphthongs turning into simple vowels. The 'th' sounds tend to turn into 'd' sounds. This is a non-rhotic accent (the 'r' are not pronounced at the end of syllable, as in RP).

California English

It is typically heard on TV and in movies. This is turning more and more into the new standard American accent – due to its popularity and media exposure. This accent often simplifies vowels and diphthongs.

Irish English

Many vowels are closer to the mouth roof. The 't' consonant is often pronounced something in-between 's' and 'sh'. The 'l' consonant is pronounced more strongly than in most English accents and has somewhat of a fuller sound to it.

Scottish English

This is a rhotic accent and, additionally, the 'r' sound is usually a rolling R. Like in Irish English, the 'l' sound is usually pronounced more strongly than in most other English accents.

Cockney

This was originally the working-class accent in London. The 'h' consonant is often silent. This is also a rhyming accent. Many expressions are transformed and extended just for the purpose of making rhymes.

"Writing" the accent

A great site to explore British accents is Whoohoo:

http://www.whoohoo.co.uk

This site lets you type in normal English text and will convert it, "translate it" as they say, in order to reflect the way the text would actually be pronounced by, for example, an Irish or Scottish person. Try it!

Adopting your own accent

Your own accent will naturally develop into the accent(s) you are exposed to the most. For example, if you are exposed to, mostly General American and Received Pronunciation, you would develop your own accent – a mix between the two.

The critical thing to keep in mind is that people need to **understand you**. Having a specific, regional, accent comes second. Note that it is also quite alright to still have an accent influenced by your native language – as long as it does not prevent people from understanding you.

As such, your job is, first and foremost, to be able to pronounce *typical* English sounds, as seen in the first part of this chapter (this is the pronunciation part). You can do this on your own, with a dictionary and some limited exposure to English dialogue. This will ensure people understand you, no matter where you are from and where they are from. (This is why this is a bad idea to practice your English with people from your own country. They will tend to have the same accent you do, so this is not a fair test of your ability to be understood by others.)

From there, secondly, you may also want to acquire a specific accent. Here, exposure is critical. For example, if you think the Southern American accents are pretty cool, expose yourself to them as much as you can and to try and pick up the accent. In doing so, you will actually also be practicing the first part (producing *only* English sounds).

Remember we have not even started with English audio at this point (TV, audio books, conversations)! Working diligently on this chapter will make communication flow and will make you benefit *much more* and *much faster*, from listening to real English.

WRAPPING IT UP

❖ Realize that you can only pronounce what you hear.

❖ Realize that pronouncing new sounds is something chiefly muscular.

❖ Try and reproduce all typical English sounds: consonants, vowels, diphthongs, and triphthongs. Try to get the position of the tongue right for vowels. Use the audio pronunciation from online dictionaries to practice.

Chapter 6

Reading

Novels and how-to books

"All books are either dreams or swords,
You can cut, or you can drug, with words."
– Amy Lowell

GOAL & EXIT

Goal

The purpose of this chapter is to help you learn a lot of vocabulary and proper English through reading. This chapter is also designed to give you the confidence that reading novels and how-to books in English provides.

Exit

This chapter is over when you have finished reading your first novel *and* your first how-to book. If you are already fairly used to reading books in English, this chapter will give you more ways to benefit from reading.

THE POWER OF READING

Filling the gap

Traditional teaching methods have put too much emphasis on using texts to learn English, often with negative consequences. **Remember, a spoken language is about speech before all else, including the text.** Schools tend to forget that for a number of reasons (the convenience of using textbooks, crowded classes, lack of interest as well as social pressures in the classroom, etc.).

We will use this chapter as a chance to capitalize on the benefits of using books, while at the same time handling their shortcomings.

Reading has the following benefits:

- Great way to learn a lot of vocabulary.
- Great way to get used to more complex phrase structures.
- Great way to self-correct, comparing what one thought and how things are actually said.
- Great means to enrich both one's culture and knowledge.

It usually comes, however, with the following shortcoming:

- Pronunciation is neglected – one does not need to pronounce properly, if at all, in order to read.

I would like to address the above shortcoming first. It is actually the opportunity to practice the previous chapter on a continuous basis and to adopt new reading habits.

Reading properly

There are mainly three ways to read: either pronouncing the text out loud; or, pronouncing the text mentally; or, not pronouncing the text at all.

For faster reading, the last option is recommended and this may be the best option in one's own native language.

However, to learn and improve your English, I recommend using the first two options exclusively -- whenever you can, read the text out loud. If you cannot (e.g., in public), pronounce the text in your head.

Reading

From the previous chapter, you are now aware of the rules with respect to pronouncing English properly. Those can be used to hear and be better understood in conversations; however, for daily practice – especially if you do not live in an English-speaking country – you should also apply them to *reading*. Here is how to proceed:

Reading text and pronouncing properly

- As you read, be careful to only pronounce sounds found in the English language, as listed in the previous chapter on phonetics.

- As much as possible, use an online dictionary to check the actual pronunciation of a word.

- In English, pronunciation and spelling rarely match. As such:

  o Be aware that adding an extra letter can change the pronunciation of a word. Compare *"bit"* and *"bite,"* *"bar"* and *"bare,"* *"hat"* and *"hate."*

  o Be aware that similar spellings may actually use different pronunciations. Compare *"flow"* and *"cow."* Also, the ending of *"wicked"* and *"moved."*

  o Be aware that all written letters are not always, pronounced. For example: *"business"* is pronounced "biz'nis," *"come"* is pronounced "kum." *"kneel"* is pronounced "neel."

  o Keep in mind that in many words, the letters 'e' and 'a' are pronounced as the mid-central vowel 'ə' (the schwa) which is almost a silent 'e.' Some words can actually fall into either this category or the previous one. (Example: *"different"* is either pronounced "diff'rent" or "diff'ə'rent")

Use an online dictionary to compare the example words.

- Within a word, part of the word is stressed while other parts are not. The same thing is true within a sentence. This is mostly to indicate what the important syllable or words are. For sentences, to emphasize properly, you need to understand what you read and especially the point of view one should adopt while reading. Otherwise, you might put the stress on different parts of the sentence, conveying different meanings, and highlight different things.

Overall, a good rule of thumb is that to pronounce or write a word properly in English, you need to have seen and heard that word *at least one time* before. There are "rules" about pronunciation and stressing the accent but there are also many, many, exceptions. As such, experience is what will make it easy for you. Remember: **the more experience you gain, the easier it becomes**. (And we will be working on that in upcoming chapters.)

Use the above technique of reading out loud or in your head as much as possible. Actually, use it all the time for your first two books. This takes more time but it will train you – not only to read properly, but to pronounce proper English automatically.

In the end, you will be able to speak English without an accent. This is well worth the investment.

YOUR FIRST NOVEL

Choosing your first novel

Too difficult a read may make you give up. I have a great technique to get started reading books in English. (Obviously, besides the one you are reading right now!)

The technique is to choose, as your first read, a book that has been made into a movie.

Great movies are often based on books, so check your top 10 favorite movies to see if that is the case.. I have included a long list in the appendix if you need examples.

Before we get started:

- Make sure this is a movie you have seen and loved. The idea is to build on your love for the movie, in order to enjoy reading the original story. (People are often disappointed when they see a movie based on a book they have loved; luckily enough, this is rarely the case the other way around.)

- If this has been a long time or you have never seen the movie, stop this chapter now and make time to watch it.

Next...

This "made into a movie" technique has the following benefits:

- **Easy focus**. As you know what the story is about, it takes less effort for you to read the book. You know what things look like, what characters to expect, the plot and so on. This is perfectly okay – and is actually preferable – when reading the book to use your memory of the actors and sets from the movie, instead of making everything up with your imagination. This way, you have fewer efforts to make regarding the story and you can use your energy to learn a lot of English.

- **Vocabulary**. As you know the story, you will be able to correctly *guess* a lot of the vocabulary you read. It is true both for descriptive vocabulary (e.g., physical descriptions, clothes, buildings, accessories) and for emotional vocabulary (feelings, attitudes, voice tone).

- **Enjoyment and achievement**. By picking a story you like and know, not only is it easier to follow and learn from the story, it is also much easier and more likely for you to actually finish the book, and enjoy doing so. Finishing your first novel in English boosts your self-confidence. It is something that you can be proud of.

Tips and tricks for reading novels

Remember that the goal throughout this method is to get you to do things totally in English, as much as possible. As such, avoid the use of a dictionary in your own language. Instead, use an English dictionary.

I understand you will not always be next to a computer as you read your novel. However, as much as possible, try to have a computer with an Internet connection handy, so you can use the techniques from chapter two, enabling you to learn quickly and easily. It will also give you the chance to check pronunciations at any time.

At this point, you should have already seen the movie you picked and have the novel handy. Go watch the movie if need be and open the book. If you have not seen the movie in a long time (you do not remember much about it – except you liked it), you may want to watch it again before we get started.

Now, let us explore more techniques for reading novels in English!

❶ Read out loud

As mentioned previously, read out loud as much as possible. If you cannot, pronounce the text in your head. Do *not* simply read quickly without pronouncing the words.

❷ Guess the meaning of words

- **Remember the movie.** For example, if in the book John Smith is said to wear a *"leather jacket,"* then recall what type of jacket he was wearing in the movie and you will know what *"leather"* means.

- An **important** word will usually be repeated throughout the book. If you do not understand it the first time around, it is okay because you will have more chances to do so later on. This means you do *not* have to look up every word in the dictionary.

- Do not start accumulating vocabulary lists. Building vocabulary lists does not help in learning foreign languages. In foreign languages, *context* is everything. **It is better to learn to guess and deal with unknown words**, than it is to build gigantic vocabulary lists. You will not have any use for vocabulary lists when talking with people. Yet, you *will* have a use for figuring things out on your own.

- Keep trying. Often time, as you proceed further with your reading, you will guess the meaning of previous words. Your goal at this point is not to know each and every word in the book. Your goal is to immerse yourself into the text in English, while having a good time!

- Do not constantly look up words in the dictionary. Try to balance having fun (*i.e.*, immersing yourself in the novel) with learning new words (pronunciation and/or meaning). You should only look words up when you know they are important but still cannot figure them out. Typically, you have seen the word quite a few times now but still cannot guess it. (If you do not have a dictionary handy, it is okay to write the word down along with the page number. This way you can check the word and its context later on.)

- **Use the context!** Context is everything. For example, if the word refers to an object, the context may let you guess what it is. Is it something one can wear? Is this something inside a room? Is it something you can hold in your hand? The genre of the book will help too. Is this a weapon? A vehicle? It is okay if you only have a blurry idea of what the word or object is, at first. This will become sharper as you keep reading!

❸ Use your "mental dictionary"

When facing an unknown word, guess the meaning of new words with what I like to call your "mental dictionary."

- See if it is a **compound word**, made of words you already know. For example, guessing the meaning of the word *"lipstick"* is fairly easy if you already know the meaning of the words "lip" and "stick."

- See if the word is **part of another word** you already know. It is like the previous technique but the other way around. For example, guessing the meaning of the word *"lid"* is not all that hard if you remember that you know the meaning of the word "eyelid."

- Notice the **etymology** of the words. Try and figure out the root of the unknown words – it may be common to other words you know. If your native language is of European origin, this can be a great help too. You will often find common roots with words in your native language.

- Similarly, is this a **special form** of a word you know? Maybe you are facing an irregular plural, or maybe in the case of verbs, this is a form you did not know about.

Not only do the above techniques help you figure out the meaning of words, they also help you to memorize them better by associations with things you already know.

This is a new habit to get into but, once you get the hang of it you will be able to figure out a lot of new vocabulary *without* any dictionary on hand. This is the art of deconstructing words and expressions and then comparing them to what you already know. Treat it as a game that you want to get good at.

❹ Idioms

- Being curious to know *how people think* in English will also help you. Idioms are a good entry door for that, as they use special expressions to illustrate a particular meaning. This is especially true about sayings (e.g., proverbs), where your native language and English may express one and the same idea using different pictures. I cannot cover all native languages here, so to get the idea: compare English sayings with sayings in your own native language (very often, the same sayings and popular wisdom exist in many, many languages). How can you use that to read more easily? When you see an idiomatic expression (*i.e.*, a special expression that illustrates a particular meaning), try and see what the expression *evokes*. From there, you can approximate the meaning. For example, if a character says: "I got it straight from the horse's mouth," he obviously did not actually speak with a horse (unless maybe if you are reading a fairy tale!), so this has to mean something else. Who did he speak to? From there, you could infer that this is just an expression and try and guess its meaning.

Vocabulary lists

Vocabulary lists are common place in language learning. I actually recommend not using them. I will explain why you should avoid them or – if you really feel that you need them – when and how to use them.

Why you should avoid vocabulary lists

- Vocabulary lists are a waste of time.
  - o Writing down all unknown words is a waste of time. You cannot remember everything. Instead, you should prioritize words that are found frequently throughout the text. (And such words can often be guessed.)
  - o Writing words down without looking up their meaning is also a waste of time. We benefit from *knowing* the words; not from merely writing them down.
  - o Looking up the word usually happens only much later. If you do not remember much about the part of the book in which it was being used, you learn less (you learn less about *how* to use the word and you have fewer means *to remember* the word). Your time is better spent looking up the word right away or trying to guess the meaning.
  - o The time spent on building vocabulary lists is better spent developing a good memory, which is not that difficult.
- It is easy to misuse vocabulary lists.
  - o Vocabulary lists are usually just single words. Single words are mostly useless because the meaning of a word does not just come from the word itself; it comes from the way it is being used. Again, this is that important idea of *context*. Most words have several meanings. The context lets you know which one is implied.

o Vocabulary lists are usually found along with the translations of the words. It is a bad habit in and of itself (more on this in the final chapter). As much as possible, you should do things 100% in English.

Do not get me wrong. It is quite okay to right words down so you do not forget to look them up. However, this should only come second to guessing the meaning, thanks to the context. This should also be limited to the most important words (based on frequency and lack of understanding).

When you write down words or expressions, you should also note the page number, so as to the review their usage and the context also, when you finally look up the word.

When and how to use vocabulary lists

If you really have to use vocabulary lists, here is how to do it. Vocabulary lists are a good thing to use if you: have a very limited amount of time, and if you need to acquire a highly specific vocabulary.

An example would be: if your company tells you that you have two weeks to prepare for a trip abroad, to investigate deforestation, but you do not know any vocabulary on that subject.

You would then carefully build a deck of vocabulary cards, with five expressions per card: on one side of the card, you would write down the words or expressions that you need to remember. On the other side, you would write their translation in your native language, or an explanation in English.

By using cards (for example, index cards or blank business cards), using one side for the words, one side for the meaning, you are then able to test yourself, which is the only good thing about it.

Please note that learning all of that vocabulary would be *faster* browsing an encyclopedia and reading about each term you need to know. This way, you would be able to remember all of the words *and* use them on the same topic. The vocabulary list then only serves as a reminder of the words you need to know and a way to test yourself.

Next?

Keep reading and, most importantly, keep enjoying your book. I will see you in the next section when you are finished reading it.

READING TO LEARN

Choose to learn like a pro

Obviously enough, all books can be said to be learning material, including novels. What we will focus on here, however, is books designed to teach you a specific skill.

Speaking English fluently is a big asset in the workplace. Beyond that, it is a big asset for learning anything you want. We will use that to our advantage in this chapter, in order to both *learn more English* (practicing) and *learn new stuff* (a new skill).

Being able to do so also legitimates adding "Technical English" or "Professional English" and "English: fluent" to your résumé. The ability to learn about a new subject by reading *in English* about it shows a greater level of fluency.

Choosing a how-to book

You have many options as to which how-to book to choose. This very book is a how-to book, in that it instructs you on how to learn English more efficiently. However, I would like you to pick a book on a different subject. Preferably, something you really would like to do and where you have to use your brains (at least a little!). This can be related to your work but does not have to be. It can be something you already know a little about or it could be a completely new topic.

Some examples would be books about: cooking, learning a musical instrument, detailed techniques for your favorite sport, financial education, self-help (such as communication, psychology...), business (such as marketing, sales...), or technology.

I often recommend self-help books because there are a lot of options there – something for everyone.

The choice is truly yours. Just make sure you pick a book in which you will *learn something new*.

Where to buy

I strongly suggest visiting Amazon.com. The ".com" site, *not* a local version. The reason being that this site offers truly the widest selection of books in English, along with many quality reviews about the books. It is also where you will find, typically, the latest editions. You might want to buy elsewhere but check Amazon.com to keep up-to-date

http://www.amazon.com

Reading how-to books

Overall, reading how-to books is the same thing as reading anything else. It may be much easier than reading a novel because you have less varied vocabulary and can focus on a specific topic. You should also apply the techniques from chapter 2 on learning faster and using the Internet. Here are some more tips.

- Learn how to pronounce the technical vocabulary. This is critical for professional books: being able to read the technical words properly will mean you have the ability and the confidence to do so – including at work. This is also important for more personal topics, as you will then feel confident discussing them with the people you meet. Keep pronouncing that vocabulary and checking it online, until you master it.

- Once you are able to pronounce all of the technical words properly, it is okay if you want to read fast and not pronounce the words out loud, or even mentally. This may actually help you to think about what you learn instead of thinking so much about the pronunciation. Check your pronunciation now and again however; to make sure that you remember it.

- How-to books are in many ways easier than novels. The vocabulary is more specific and less varied. However, words, as such, also carry more meaning. There is a *higher price to pay* for not understanding a word properly. Because of that, look up any word you are not sure of.

- Wikipedia's hyperlinks are your friends to quickly navigate through related words and concepts and master the technical vocabulary quickly.

You are starting to think in English

By reading a book that teaches you something, you are already starting to *think* in English.

Be sure to **use the ideas you learn about** as you read. This means applying what you learn and even just thinking about them. Try to *visualize* the ideas you read about. This will make them more real. Once in a while, think about how everything you have learned is connected. Doing so will train your memory on the topic and will make it easier for you to talk about it.

By making conscious effort to think in English and by focusing on a specific topic, you will soon feel **comfortable thinking about that topic** – ideas will come naturally to you on the subject.

For example, if you are reading a book on learning the guitar, you would visualize the different parts of your instrument as you read about them (the guitar neck; the strings; the frets, etc.). Similarly, you would start calling the musical notes by their English names, instead of the names used in your native language. You would then try to use this knowledge as you read or as you practice the instrument. This way, the knowledge would really *stick* in your memory and you would be able to think about the subject in English a little already. The more you do it, the bigger those English ideas grow and the easier it gets. You then become able to discuss them naturally.

More about all this in the final chapter until then, you know what? You can actually **feel good about yourself** for finishing a novel, a how-to book, plus the fact you are starting to think in English!

WRAPPING IT UP

❖ Get used to properly pronouncing the text you read, be it out loud or mentally. This will build a *very strong foundation* for speaking English well.

❖ Read your first novel in English. Use the opportunity to learn a lot of vocabulary and about phrase structures and proper English syntax, while still improving your pronunciation

❖ Read your first how-to book in English. Make sure you pronounce the more technical vocabulary perfectly. Use the opportunity to start *thinking* in English, by connecting all that you learn and reflecting on it.

Chapter 7

TV

Learn English while watching TV!

"Television is the first truly democratic culture – the first culture available to everybody and entirely governed by what the people want. The most terrifying thing is what people do want."
– Clive Barnes

GOAL & EXIT

Goal

This is one of the most important chapters in this book. Mastering it will make you fluent in English for life. The goal of this chapter is to make you *comfortable* watching TV in English. This lets you learn and practice English every day without stress.

Exit

Once you feel confident you can keep watching TV series in English without subtitles and still have fun, you can move on to the next chapter.

This would round up to having watched all available episodes from at least two TV shows (count at least 5 seasons per show), preferably sitcoms. However, unless you like nothing at all on TV, you should never stop practicing this chapter, as this is one of the main keys to becoming bilingual.

TV AS A WAY TO PRACTICE

Bad press

TV gets a lot of bad press. People watch it too much. People blame it for making kids fat, lazy and stupid. If you ask me, a lot of parents thought they could just let their kids sit in front of the TV, sort of like having a new babysitter, but it just does not work that way. You have everything on TV, good or bad. That being said, most people watch (a lot) of TV and we *can* use that time to learn a lot of English!

Learning is like traveling

The great thing about TV is you can use it to bring foreign countries to your living room (or to your computer or bedroom) instead of having to travel to those foreign countries.

Do not get me wrong, traveling is great and most of us, including yours truly, would love to spend many years, if not their lives, doing so. However, this is not always convenient or practical.

My point here is that, with TV, you can practice *real* and *interesting* (or, at least, entertaining) **spoken English every day**. I do not care how you watch it (satellite channels, DVD, legal downloads…), just do what is convenient for you. I will call all of it *TV* for the sake of simplicity.

WHAT TO WATCH TO LEARN THE MOST

Making things easy, yet efficient

Once you feel comfortable watching TV in English, without any subtitles, then please feel free to watch whatever you like –

be it series, whatever the genre, movies, talk shows, or documentaries – whatever; you choose.

Until then, to get you started watching TV, there is one type of programming I ask you to use: **sitcoms**.

Sitcoms help you learn English

Sitcoms, for "situational comedies" (i.e.: series like *Friends, Malcolm in the Middle, Seinfeld, How I Met Your Mother…*) come as the most recommended type of TV program for a number of reasons:

- They are short. With about 20 minutes on average per episode, it does not take too much effort to get started and it is very easy to make time for them, even in a busy schedule. You can also conveniently extend a session with more episodes as time allows.
- Sitcoms are all about two things: dialogue and visuals.
  - Dialogue. You will be exposed to a lot of talking, usually in a pretty theatrical way: actors tend to articulate properly, lines tend to be short and to the point, and punch lines let you check you understood what just happened. **You are exposed to some real, yet rather easy English.**
  - Visuals. Half of the fun in a sitcom comes from the situation the characters are in and you can usually understand it just by watching. What you see on-screen is not just there for decorative purposes, it really *serves* the program. You could turn off the soundtrack and still understand a lot. This means you will **understand a lot intuitively** (and still be able to make the link with the dialogue you are hearing) and that you will still **enjoy yourself, even if you do not understand everything**.

- Sitcoms are often about **everyday life**. You will learn a lot of useful vocabulary. Also, as you go on about your day, this increases the chances of you thinking again about the show you watched last night, which means it makes you think in, and about, English more.

Additionally, watching something fun is a great way to learn. It takes a lot of the **stress out of the equation**. Running jokes get you playing along with the characters: you start trying to guess what they are going to say next. Not understanding what the characters said, but still having a laugh (because of the situation) also builds your **curiosity**. The more curious you are, the easier it is to focus. Have you ever laughed or started smiling with your friends because everyone was laughing, yet you did not hear the whole thing? Didn't you just want so badly to know what had been said? Well, the same situations occur while watching sitcoms.

TV series in general

TV series, overall, including sitcoms, are a great way to learn.

Following the same characters in episode after episode, makes it really easy to get used to the way they speak. You repeatedly *tune in* to the way each character speaks: individual pronunciation, voice tone, rhythm, and figures of speech. You get used to both the character and to the actor. This is critical in learning to speak fluently. Realize this: your ability to understand English as easily as your native language will come in many ways **one person at a time**. You *learn an accent* one person at a time. As you grow used to someone's way of speaking, even on camera, you grow used to the thousands of people who will speak the same way, but you need to start with *one* person who speaks that way. Season after season, you grow intimately acquainted with the accent.

Finally, you have a whole season to understand what is happening on the show. Compare this to a movie, where you only have about two hours to get used to the plot, actors, and characters. TV series are easier to understand. You can fine tune your understanding of the show, as time goes by, episode after episode. It is easy to make it a habit.

WHAT YOU NEED

A recap of what you need

You quite simply need to find a sitcom you like and you need the original English version *without* subtitles. **No subtitles at all**, not in English, not in your native language – nothing! This is important, even critical, to making progress here. Trust me: you can do it, you will make progress that way and you will have a good time also.

You need a number of episodes. Having at least three seasons is recommended but five would be the best. This is simply for the sake of simplicity. You do not want to stop practicing your English just because you are running out of episodes.

This is perfectly okay if you want to start with a sitcom you have already seen before. It is even recommended if you consider your spoken English to be still really poor. This way, you will not have to bother about the plot too much and can guess much of the vocabulary. Just make sure it is a show you still enjoy.

Finally, I have included a selection in the appendix. Sitcoms that come both recommended for their English and are fairly easy to find. (Please note I have not included cartoons in it. Watching real people talk is a better way to learn pronunciation.)

Where to get it

Depending on where you live, it can be more or less easy to get the TV shows you want in English without subtitles. For now, DVDs seem to be the easiest legal way to do so. To save a lot of money, consider renting. The original version is usually included on the DVD – the question then simply becomes whether you can remove the subtitles or not – you will have to try it for yourself.

Downloads on Peer-to-Peer networks, such as BitTorrent and eDonkey, are pretty popular – people record the shows on American TV and then share them on the Internet. This may be legal to watch in some countries, when and if this is a new show whose rights have not been licensed in your country yet. This is by no means legal advice. I am not a lawyer, so please consult your local laws.

Things are slowly evolving. As frontiers tend to disappear it should be easier (hopefully) to legally watch new TV shows from abroad. I have summed up all available options at the time of writing in the appendix. There are now some great options for watching American and British channels from abroad. Be sure to check out the appendix.

DVD region codes

Shopping abroad can be the chance to get more options. However, DVDs are region-protected, which means they are designed to only play on a DVD player enabled for the same region. Here is a short list of the "region codes" and their associated countries. The country code is usually displayed on the DVD itself *and* in the product description on shopping sites.

Region Code Number : Area

1: USA; Canada, including Québec.

2: Japan; Europe; South Africa; Middle East; Egypt.

3: South East Asia; East Asia, including Hong Kong.

4: Australia; New-Zealand; Latin America.

5: Russia and former Soviet Union; India; Africa.

6: China.

There are also DVDs with region code 0 or ALL. Those can be played on *any* DVD player.

For your information, Amazon UK [http://www.amazon.co.uk] sells mostly region-2 DVDs and Amazon.com [http://www.amazon.com] sells mostly region-1 DVDs (though each site will also sell DVDs from other regions, in their "Import" department or similar).

UNDERSTANDING SITCOMS

OK, so you are about to discover a show you like in its true form: you will hear the actors' *real* voices; you will learn the *authentic* dialogue and word play. Moreover, you do not have to feel bad about watching TV anymore – you are *working on your English*!

Please make sure you will not be disrupted for the next 40 minutes. Sitcoms will usually take you the time of the episode but, for this first session, we will go more slowly.

❶ **First sessions**

- **Lend your ear** to the TV show. You might not be used to hearing English dialogue all that much so this is normal if this feels awkward at first; you will go over it. Focus on the sound and try and apply the phonetics principles you learned in chapter 5. You have seen the theory. You are now putting it into practice.

- **Repeat the words** you hear to compare what you think you have heard with how one would pronounce it. The idea here is to check if you got it right. Did you hear right? Can you pronounce it right? Basically, you are applying what you have learned about phonetics.

  o **Review chapter 5** (on phonetics) as you watch your first few episodes.

  o Repeat the **most important words** and at first, all the words you *know* that you understand. The goal is proper pronunciation.

  o You will know if you got the pronunciation right by **comparing** how you pronounce it with how they say it on the show. Check again if what they say on the show and how you pronounce it sounds similar. Make sure that you are only using 100% English sounds.

- The whole idea at this point is to **"tune-in."** You are used to hearing voices in your native language; you are now adapting, "tuning in", to hearing (and pronouncing) in English. You need to adjust.

- The sound may seem scrambled at first. It may seem as if what you hear is sort of blurry and you need to make it sharper. Basically, this can be pretty chaotic. How do you go around it?

  o Your understanding will increase in multiple ways, **hour after hour, week after week**. The core concept here is to observe and be focused. This will **turn the initial chaos into clear sound units**. Your brain and ears will adapt.

  o The **words you do recognize** will support the rest. It is normal and perfectly okay to *not* understand everything at first. Focus on what you do understand. This will provide a structure upon which to build. Imagine having a puzzle game where most pieces are missing but some are visible and in the right place. You would then be able to get an idea of the whole picture, despite the missing pieces. It is the same here, with sound. The words you do understand will open the door to new sounds and additional new words.

- You may feel uncomfortable at first watching TV shows, just because you do not understand everything. As human beings, we feel a need to understand. Not understanding, even a mere TV show, may feel awkward and disturbing. This is alright and this *will* go away soon. Take it as if traveling: if you travel in a foreign country where you do not know the people, the places and do not understand what is being said, you may feel **homesickness**. You get over it by growing used to the foreign country (which is not so foreign anymore then) and by building relationships, as well as new, comfortable habits. Growing used to the TV show, episode by episode, will help. Talking with your friends and family about the fact you watch TV shows in English will also make it more casual and will help you keep to your schedule (instead of feeling awkward, you will feel proud).

- Realize you can **learn from pictures** in several ways:

  o You try and **guess the meaning** of what is happening on screen. This is as if there was no sound. You learn from what you see.

  o You try and **make links** (correlations) between what you see on screen and the words you hear. You use your mind to bridge the gap between visual information and auditory information, even if you do not hear clearly.

  o A study on communication concluded that communication is 55% body language (posture and other gestures), 38% voice tone (the quality and inflections of a person's voice) and only 7% the actual words spoken. Now, not all studies agree on those numbers but the fact that **nonverbal communication contributes to most of the communication** is agreed upon. This means that, as you watch a foreign program, even without understanding all of the spoken words, **you will still understand most of the communication going on**. This makes it easy to keep on watching the show. From there, it is only natural that you will associate what you see with what you hear and start developing your verbal understanding.

- Accept the fact that you will understand only a limited part of the dialogue at first. **This will increase with time and practice.** If you understand 50% of the words at first, then your goal will be to understand 60% in the coming days, and so on. Some people have a hard time accepting that: they want to understand everything right away or else would rather give it up. Remember you are on a time-constraint when watching a TV show: you can only understand so much of the flow of words coming on… You may be lagging behind that flow at first and this is, actually, to be expected – this is perfectly normal. Episode after episode, you will get closer and closer to understanding things "live", right away, and one day soon, you will be in synchronization with the flow of the dialogue. Your confidence will also naturally expand in the process. It does not take genius or power, it merely takes time.

❷ **Day after day**

Here are several tips to help you make the most out of this exercise:

- Your goal is to experience **"Aha" moments**. I am talking about those times where you will be excited because you have finally understood something that was there all along. "Oh! He says the word <Blah Blah>! I get it!". This is your ears opening and your brain growing used to the new language. You can help it by being focused and checking on your phonetics lesson seriously once in a while.

- You have to **trust the sound you hear**. Most education nowadays is text-based. There are no texts here. You need to get used to learning from sound and voices.

- **Focus: use your ear and your sight and your mind to**

figure out the most of what you see. You can take it like a detective game.

- **Be proud of yourself.** Take pride in taking big steps. You are entering new territory and are learning a lot. You are learning to figure things out and do things 100% in English. Not so many people do that. Additionally, watching TV shows is one of the major two steps in speaking great and fluent English. So, be proud of what you are doing, you will be speaking better English than most soon enough!

- Realize that there is a **warm-up period** when watching TV shows, just like there may be for sports or musical instruments. If you have not watched any TV show for a while, your first minutes, or even your first few episodes, will be dedicated to growing used to the actors' accents again. On a personal note: if I have not been practicing my English for weeks (which is rare but can happen) I myself need to get back into it, even though I am as comfortable speaking American English as I am my native language nowadays. I may feel disconnected for the first few episodes on a TV show, but this will fade away naturally after a while. This is a natural warm-up process. At some point, however, you will not need to go through any warm-up time at all (except maybe after long breaks), as English becomes a normal and daily part of your life.

- As you get further and further into the show, you may want to start using the rewind function. At first you should *not* use it, because this will spoil your enjoyment of the show and you already have a lot to try and understand (on the first episodes, you will simply understand what you can and every piece of dialogue is a chance to learn. Rewinding would take ages and not help you at all). However, **as time goes, this is best to**

become more careful about your understanding. When you feel you can understand something like 95% of the dialogue, then you should start using rewind in order to reach 100% of understanding. If you are watching your TV shows on a computer: several video player programs let you go back just a few seconds at the press of a key, making it easier to hear a word again several times. (For example, on Windows, you can use MPCStar [http://www.mpcstar.com].)

- Warning: **do not try to translate** what you hear. Your goal is to understand right away; use the shortest path so to speak. You want to see the meaning (*e.g.*, mental pictures) of the dialogue right away, without translating and going through your native language first.

- Do you think this is **too hard** and no fun, even after a week or so?

  o See **"The two weeks switch"** below.

  o **Try watching replays**. After about two weeks, watch one or two of the first episodes, the very first ones you saw 100% in English. This should help you realize that you *have made* progress. When we do something every day, we do not see ourselves changing Going back helps us realize just how much we have accomplished.

  o If this is all really too hard, **try using English subtitles by turning them ON and then back OFF**. Do not keep them on all the time. Just make use of them for the words you do not understand. Let me insist on that. You need to decide whether you are watching the TV show to focus and learn (and still have fun) or if you are using it *only* to have fun (chill out, relax). To focus and learn, you need to turn on the subtitles only on specific words. If this is all still too hard, maybe you have burned through the material too fast. Go back and practice previous chapters to learn more vocabulary.

❸ Making it all natural

- As you progress into the series, just make sure you **have a good time and learn**. Learning watching TV show is, overall, a pretty natural process. Daily exposure lets your subconscious mind adapt and figure out a lot of things (see "The two weeks switch" below).

- **Watch a complete TV show series before moving on** to a new one. This way, you really push your understanding of the actors' various accents to the max *and* can enjoy a nice feeling of accomplishment. Next, I suggest moving on to a new sitcom. Stick with the sitcoms – they are very visual, good fun, easy to watch… This makes it easy, and rather fast, to learn a lot. Get used to a second sitcom and to all of its characters, actors, and universe.

- After that, start watching **other shows and/or movies** to your liking. Get used to new accents and new ways of speaking. By then, watching TV to learn English should have become pretty much a new habit and you are free to do anything you want with it. ☺

A word on learning

"*Most learning and change takes place at the unconscious level.*" This is a quote from Bandler and Grinder's *Frogs into Princes*, a seminal book on psychology. I believe this strongly applies to learning languages in general, and especially using the methods described in this book. Languages are learned through exposure, mental associations, and practice. You do not need to actively think about everything you do in order to learn a language. Sure, conscious efforts are required for grammar, phonetics, or to start something new. However, this conscious effort is typically required only to get started. Once the right habits are in place, all learning happens automatically, without much conscious effort. From what I have observed, this is the same thing with learning TV or listening to audio books and most other ways to practice English to learn English.

My point is this: getting into a new habit requires effort and focus... Once that habit is in place, you do not need to provide much effort anymore; meanwhile, you keep reaping the benefits from the new habit!

The two weeks switch

In my experience, something happens after about two weeks into the practice of watching TV – again, sitcoms are the best example. After this amount of time, **the efforts needed to keep practicing seem to disappear**, making it all the more easy and enjoyable. Basically, after about two weeks, watching a sitcom in English without subtitles becomes as natural and enjoyable, if not more, as watching it dubbed or subtitled in your native language.

It does *not* mean that you will understand everything or that English becomes as easy as your native language. This means that **it then takes no effort to practice your English**, no effort at all. (This is why I recommend sitcoms so much If you can find a fun, enjoyable way to practice your English *every day*, you win; and, after about two weeks, sitcoms are *exactly* that.)

I am not certain where this comes from, though I suspect the ears and mind finally adapt to the new English sounds after about that time. Also, I suspect this is roughly the time required to grow used to figuring out the vocabulary, or, at least, handling the vocabulary you do not know without spoiling your fun.

This is just a rough number and it has a lot to do with the frequency of your practice – this is why I suggest an episode a day, at least, to start with.

Do me a favor, will you? Try it for several weeks and let me know by e-mail how long it took *you* before you could watch your favorite TV show without effort. (My e-mail is at the end of the introduction.)

FILMS

What if you do not like TV shows? Well then, you are really missing out on a great way to practice daily using something entertaining, where you can hear real English.

I do not recommend movies as much as I do TV shows because switching from one movie to the next leaves you no time to get used to the actors' accents and to the vocabulary. Let us compare numbers: a movie is about 2 hours long... A sitcom, with just 20 minutes per episode, 22 episodes per season and 5 seasons is already 36 hours... In 36 hours you can *really* get used to an accent!

That being said, it is of course better to watch a movie in English than in your own language. Moreover, you will get the chance to be exposed to new accents.

Here are a few tips just for movies:

Movie time

- When you go to the movies and, hence, cannot remove the subtitles, to prevent reading them: try to focus your attention elsewhere. What works is focusing your attention on the actors' eyes or mouth, this way you will not look at the bottom of the screen.

- At home, this is okay if you want to turn the English subtitles back on at first. Getting used to a movie is harder than a sitcom because you have less time. A good idea is to just use the remote to turn the subtitles on and off, and rewind, as needed.

- Try watching a movie or two with the "English for the hearing impaired" option turned on (on DVDs). This way, you will learn some vocabulary on how to describe the action going on. Just try it and you will see what I mean.

- Most tips that work for TV shows also work for movies. To make your life easier, just make sure you start watching movies in English seriously *only* after you are totally comfortable with a couple of TV shows. Also keep in mind it takes more energy to watch a 2-hours long movie than it does a few episodes from a TV show.

WRAPPING IT UP

❖ Start watching a sitcom, at least one episode a day, every day. Watch more as time allows.

❖ Try it for a few weeks, totally in English, without subtitles. You will realize that you can adapt to it and have a really good time every day watching TV *and* practicing your English.

❖ Move on to the next chapter once you have watched at least *two* complete TV series (count 5 seasons per TV show).

❖ Stick to this program to maintain and expand your English, without effort, every day or so.

Chapter 8

Audio books

Lifelong learning

"The hearing ear is always found close to the speaking tongue."
– Ralph Waldo Emerson

GOAL & EXIT

Goal

The goal here (hear? ☺) is for you to hear English daily and start thinking in English. You should have a good knowledge of phonetics and be comfortable watching TV shows before you get started.

Exit

Audio books are the best tool to maintain your English – they help you maintain and expand your vocabulary, your listening skills and even your ability to speak English – there is nothing else like it. As such, listening to audio books should become a lifelong habit and there is no reason to stop once you start.

For the purpose of this book: you can move on to the next chapter once you are used to the voice of at least two different narrators. After that, you should keep listening to audio books to keep your English skills sharp!

ABOUT AUDIO BOOKS

What is an audio book? Not everyone is familiar with this format so let me describe it briefly.

An audio book is, quite simply, a book in audio format, that is to say, a regular book read out loud by someone and available as a recording. Audio books used to be available on tapes, next on CDs and are now available as downloadable files.

The best way to listen to an audio book would certainly be in MP3 format. This way, you can listen to it anywhere and on any device (portable MP3 player, computer, most mobile phones). The second best format would be the CD, because, this way, you know you can listen to it on many different devices also. (My point is this: try to stay away from audio books in unusual file formats. Usually, you will not be able to listen to those on any device you want and this may quickly become annoying.)

Enough with the formats — let us talk about the content.

Audio books are available mainly for two types of books: self-help books and novels.

I highly recommend listening to self-help books. The main reason is that this is a very lively genre, in many respects. For starters, narrators for those books are usually also the author of the book, so they really get into what they are saying and speak with passion. Self-help is also a lot about learning and thinking about what you hear/read; as such, they make you more of an active listener than a novel would. Basically, self-help books will get you involved in what you are listening and this will, in turn, help you think in English.

Novels are okay to listen to but they will make you much more of a passive listener. As such, I do not recommend them as a starting point.

CHOOSING AN AUDIO BOOK

As we have just seen, it is better to start with a self-help book. "Self-help" can refer to a variety of books, and I will take it in its broadest sense, as any book meant to teach you something and improve your life – be it personal or professional.

As such, this will cover areas as broad as psychology, relationships, communication, business, money... I will also include anything educational and "how-to" books in that category, so if you come across, for example, a great audio book about learning a new music skill, and that is what you want to do, then please go for it.

It may not always be easy to choose. If you are running short on ideas, simply try to pick a best-seller in psychology, communication, or finance to get you started.

Please, also take the time to listen to samples of the audio book before buying, so you know that you like the narrator's voice.

Buyer's Guide

Where to buy audio books

iTunes [http://www.apple.com/itunes]

If you own an iPod or an iPhone, buying on the iTunes store can be a good idea. However, at the time of writing, the audio books are only available in M4B format, a format that is only readable with Apple software (iTunes or an iPod, iPhone or iPad) and with no sign of making those books available as MP3 downloads. If you want to convert those files into MP3, you will have to burn them onto a CD and, from there, rip the CD into MP3 files (which is just plain silly). Do *not* buy from iTunes if you want to be able to play your files on a non-Apple device.

Audible [http://www.audible.com]

Audible is a company that specializes in audio books. However, once again, the files come in a proprietary format, which means you cannot read them on any device you want. Audible supports a number of devices, from multimedia players to mobile phones. If you buy there, make sure the devices you want to listen the audio book on are supported. Here, also, you may burn the files onto a CD and then rip the CD into MP3 files. This is now an Amazon company and you will find that downloadable audio books on Amazon actually redirect to Audible.

Amazon [http://www.amazon.com]

As mentioned above, all audio book downloads at Amazon are actually handled by Audible. Amazon is good if you want to buy audio books on CD. You will also find MP3 files on CD but the choice is limited. Please note: self-help books and similar are currently located in the "Health, Mind & Body" sections, in the "Audiobooks" department.

Please take the time to see which of the above options you prefer and keep on with this chapter once you have an audio book handy.

With no sensible option to get audio books as MP3 files legally, there are also, not surprisingly, a lot of audio books being shared on Peer-to-Peer networks. This will hopefully end up being a strong signal for companies to make those available on MP3 legally.

Free audio books!

You can find hundreds of classics, mostly novels, for free on those two sites:

http://www.booksshouldbefree.com A site very easy to navigate with hundreds of audio books for free. They use books from the LibriVox project.

http://librivox.org The project responsible for bringing these classics for free as audio books.

UNDERSTANDING AN AUDIO BOOK

Similar to working on the phone, listening to an audio book is a true test of your English skills. No visuals to help you out, nor gestures, nor expressions; all you have is your ability to decode sound into something meaningful.

Overall, everything you have learned in the previous chapters will come in handy as you listen to your first audio books. Knowing the English sounds (phonetics) will prove immensely valuable. Being able to handle situations where you do not know all the words will be useful (like when you watch TV). Being able to think about what you learn will also prove a big help (like when you read how-to books).

Tips to listen to audio books

- You should know the vocabulary used in the book. You may learn a few new words (see below) but, mostly, you should know the area of expertise of the book. This is why I recommend using self-help or educational audio books, as those will usually be books about topics you are already know about.

- As such, listening to an audio book becomes a process of reacquainting yourself with how the vocabulary is pronounced. It is merely like applying what you have learned on phonetics, except this time you are going at full speed.

- A word you did not understand?

  o If the word matters really, it will be repeated again later on and you will get a new chance to recognize it.

  o Try repeating the word to yourself to see if it helps. Can you make out the syllables?

  o The "Rewind" function is your friend. This may be more convenient to listen to audio books on a computer at first, because the rewind function is usually more convenient, and because you can then use an online dictionary more easily.

  o Think about the fact that you may actually know the word you are hearing. Maybe, you just do not know that it is actually how the word is supposed to be pronounced.

  o Finally, if you still cannot figure out the word, try to figure out the different ways it could be spelled and look it up in a dictionary, preferably online (to listen to the pronunciation given by the dictionary). There are only a limited number of ways the words you hear could be spelled.

- Do not try to figure out how everything you hear is spelled. The purpose of audio books to learn English is that you may finally give up on text and focus on your listening skills. As you grow better at this, you will be able to understand English right away and it is preparing you to meet people in person.

It is quite normal if you find audio books to be pretty hard to understand at first. The goal is for you to get better at it. That is why they are so good for your practice. You are finally confronting yourself to something as difficult as a native speaker of English, going at full speed.

If you only understand 50% of what you hear at first, this is okay. Focus on what you understand. Live with it – accept that you do not understand everything at first. Even if you are now good at understanding TV shows, you will need some time to get used to audio books, as they are faster and provide more content The basis you have now will then expand: your listening skills will vastly improve and those 50%, for example, will turn into understanding 60%, 70% and so on, until you truly understand anything you listen to.

As you grow used to someone's voice, along with his specific pronunciation and accent, you will gain a new sense of confidence. For maybe the first time, you will feel totally confident with the way someone, who is a native English speaker, speaks. This is a major step and prepares you to speak English most fluently.

The next step is quite simply to try listening to a new narrator. Also get used to his or her voice. As recommended, get used to at least two different narrators before attacking the next chapter. This simply means finishing two audio books.

After that, every new book will be like meeting someone new. You may very well grow fond of discovering new accents (in the sense that everybody has a slightly different accent, even when two persons were born and raised in the same place).

You may also find that this helps you tremendously in understanding the people you meet and/or watching TV and films.

Using this audio book strategy to learn, in general, and to maintain your English, in particular, will prove immensely valuable for you, both personally and professionally. What is more, you can – and should – **listen to audio books anywhere**: on the go, jogging or working out, around the house, sitting in waiting rooms... It is a huge asset: you are using otherwise wasted time and turning it into useful time that enriches your life.

WRAPPING IT UP

❖ Pick a self-help audio book.

❖ Get used to the narrator's specific voice – his pronunciation, his accent.

❖ Think about what you hear and learn.

❖ Get used to at least two different narrators.

❖ Keep using audio books in order to learn and to maintain better English for life.

Chapter 9

Meeting people
Making it all lively

"Strangers are friends you have yet to meet."
– Anonymous

GOAL & EXIT

Goal

Speak with native speakers and do so regularly.

Exit

Meeting and chatting with native speakers should, of course, become a lifelong habit. For the purpose of this book, you may move on to the next chapter once you have met with at least 10 native speakers and held in-depth conversations.

PREPARATION

Everything you have done until now, while applying this book, has been in preparation for this moment. You have been building your skills, gaining experience on how proper – yet real – English is spoken. You have all the tools, now is the time to use them in a "live" setting.

Meeting your first few people in English, in person, is at the same time exciting and daunting. Exciting because this is what you have been longing for from the start: meeting people to actually speak English!... Daunting because this is a moment of truth – you will realize all that you still have to work on.

Your preparation should have built a strong knowledge of syntax, a vast vocabulary, and a strong understanding of phonetics, to both speak and listen. Now, you will get the chance to use them all together.

Also keep something in mind: you are *still* learning. The strong foundation you have built is a resource. Now, your job is to get in the habit of speaking in English. This may feel uncomfortable at first. You may feel like your ability to speak is weak, but with practice, it will quickly improve and soon become natural – as if the language was your own. ☺

HAVING FUN MEETING NEW PEOPLE

A lot of people want to improve their English for work. It is a worthy goal, however, you should keep in mind that the more relaxed you are doing something, the better you are at it. Moreover, as mentioned throughout this book, the more fun you have doing something, the more you will want to do it again. Besides, starting to speak English at work can be too restrictive. You want to be able to express yourself freely, without fear of judgment, in order to get your words flowing.

For those reasons, I think it is critical that you go out in your spare time (either in your own town or abroad) to meet people who are native English speakers.

This section will give you tips on meeting native speakers.

Where to meet native speakers

MeetUp and Facebook

MeetUp [http://www.meetup.com] is a great website to meet people with the same interests. The site is designed for people to create and host events, usually in small groups, at the host's place or publicly. Most events are free or require a ridiculously low entry fee. Just visit the website and pick an activity you like to see if people are planning events on the subject in English (most users of the site are English speakers).

As Facebook [http://www.facebook.com] has grown immensely popular, it has also become something of a competition for MeetUp. As such, you should also look for Facebook events, in English, in your area.

Small ads, magazines and "expat" websites

Try and find where expatriates post their small ads in your city. Big cities often have a dedicated magazine just for expatriates. You may also want to try the Internet, as any big city is pretty sure to have a dedicated website just for English-speaking expatriates.

Once you have found it, you will get access to a lot of information as to where people meet in your city and on special events with mostly English-speaking people. Do yourself a favor, start visiting those places regularly and participating.

Traveling

Any time you travel abroad there is a great opportunity to meet with tourists from English-speaking countries.

You will also get the chance to practice your English with non-native speakers, of course, but try to practice with native speakers as much as possible. Speaking with non-native speakers has a tendency to force you into using only limited vocabulary and casts a doubt any time the other person uses a fancy word ("Did he just use an expression I did not know about or is it bad English?").

You may also want to *kill two birds with one stone* and meet with any friend you have made online during chapter 3.

Finally, choosing to spend your holidays in an English-speaking country makes a lot of sense. Remember, meeting people is supposed to be fun! This can be a great way to relax and makes for great memories.

WORK

As you gain experience and confidence in English, you should start being able to help with anything English in your company.

Depending on your position, you may or may not be required to speak English already. If you are, then now is your chance to take the lead, since you will be speaking better English than most people (assuming you have applied yourself to all of the previous chapters). If you are not, then now is your chance to be proactive and help out, in English, whenever the need arises. Do not ask if you can help; just help: people who speak poor English, in your company, will be glad you did.

Depending on your personality, you may or may not feel comfortable doing any of the above. You may also start doubting yourself. Maybe you can watch TV in English, but how good does that make you for business and people in real-life? This is pretty natural. We are often too hard on ourselves. Stop panicking and just acknowledge your actual **experience** in the matter. If you can watch TV in English, keep up a conversation, and write in that language, then you definitely *are* a huge asset to your company.

If there is no need at all to speak English in your company at any level, then maybe now is your chance to change jobs, use your English skills and thereby get a pay raise.

A lot of the above does not have to do with English itself, but merely with the fact that companies require us to take the lead and sell ourselves more and more.

Remember one thing: if you have reached this point in the book, applying yourself to what you read, then you have acquired a lot more ease speaking English. As such, you will have a really good time **doing something new, and doing it in English** – in your company or in a new company. So just go for it!

ON THE PHONE

Be it for fun or for work, most meetings in-person will usually be arranged, or require you to be on the phone at some point. Here are a few pointers to help you to feel more comfortable.

The most useful thing on the phone is to be prepared with specific ways of saying things. When you are on the phone, you do not have the time to look up words or expressions online or in a dictionary. Time seems to go faster because you do not have much time, if any, to put things on hold and look up what you need. Preparation is key.

Here are some expressions that will come in handy.

On the phone

The person you are calling is not available at the moment? Try those:

- *"When is the best time to call?"*
- *"Do you know when she will be back?"*
- *"May I leave a message?"*

Missed a word or did not quite understand something? Try those:

- *"I'm sorry, I did not get that. Could you repeat please?"*
- *"I'm sorry, what did you just say?"*
- *"I'm sorry, come again?."*
- *"When did you say we could meet?"*
- *"What did you say was the best time to call?"*

Need to write something down perfectly? Try this. This is a must-have for surnames and other proper names (*e.g.,* places).

- *"How do you spell that please?"*

You should be able to verify that you understood correctly or recapitulate (for example, at the end of the conversation):

- *"If I understand correctly, you mean that..."*
- *"If I get that right, you mean that..."*

IN PERSON

· How you behave when you meet new people depends on your character. The tips below are merely here to help you be more comfortable when that happens. The goal is for you to have a good time, to get what you want if in a work setting, and to keep the conversation flowing.

The first few times you meet people, even if you do great on the activities mentioned in this book (audio books and chatting online, to name a couple), it is quite alright if you make mistakes and do not feel comfortable. It is part of the game. It is a new game, and you will get better at it and more confident with practice.

Do not try to be perfect. After training for months, maybe hours a day to improve your English, it is only natural that you want to do well and make a good impression. However, keep in mind that the main goal of communication is for it to work both ways. If you think too much – and this is what happens when you try to be perfect, it will not work so well. Just try to let the words flow out of your mouth naturally; do not think too much. **It is better to say something wrong and correct yourself afterward**, than it is to over-think and speak too little. Keep in mind that you get better as you practice, and this means *talking!*

Do not switch to your mother tongue. If other people who speak your native language are there, it is tempting to switch back to your native language. Do not do this, this is all especially important in the early days, the first few times you go out (you should only speak your native language if you need to translate for others). Similarly, if you do not know or remember how to say something, do not bother mentioning what the word for it is, in your native language, as this brings no value and is only confusing to people. Instead, use another word, or,quite simply, **explain what the word you are looking for is, and the people you talk to will be happy to help** (this way, either you remember the word, or you learn a new one).

Be open about your situation. Honesty goes a long way. Ask people to correct you when you say something that just is not quite correct English, or if you mispronounce a word.

People will usually be very willing to help. Native English-speakers have less of an incentive to learn foreign languages, since everyone else learns English, so they often are pretty humble about foreign languages and pretty glad they can help.

Now, what exactly should you do to *understand* what is going on and *keep your own words flowing* during the interactions?

Meeting your first speakers

To enjoy yourself, you need both to understand others and to express yourself. If one or the other is not quite right, you will feel bad about the situation.

<u>In order to understand people:</u>

- It is better and easier to get used to one person at a time. Be polite with people and their group. Obviously, try to meet everyone, but **seize the opportunities to speak one-on-one.**

- **Tune-in to the other person's accent.** Remember, when you start a new TV show or audio book, this may take you a little while to adapt yourself to the accent, correct? Well, the same thing occurs with people. So what do you do in the meantime? When you do not understand what the person says, especially early on in the conversation, ask the person to repeat the words you do not understand and repeat after them. Then explain to them: *"I just need to get used to your own personal accent... Everyone has his own accent, no matter how slight. So this is las if I am tuning in.. Like a radio..."*. The other person will usually find it funny and this can start conversations about several topics (accents, languages, origins, meeting people). It also states that you just need some time to adapt and that things will get easier and easier. This is much better than asking the other person to speak slowly, because the way mentioned above, you remain on even ground with the other person *and* bring something to the conversation. This is better than asking the other person for efforts and turning the conversation into sort of a one-way language exchange.

<u>In order to let your words out easily and speak smoothly:</u>

- The less you think the better it is, *really*. **Your goal here is to be spontaneous** and have a conversation (it is not to mentally rehearse your grammar or any other linguistic details). So do not think; instead, just say what is on your mind and have a good time doing so! People love for others to be spontaneous. You may wonder what happens when you stop thinking about what you say... Well, the good thing is that your subconscious takes over; you go in "autopilot", so to speak. This is a good thing, a great thing actually, since we want to be able to use the English language naturally.

- Try and **use expressions you have heard before, on TV or in audio books** (this is why those are better than reading to learn English: when you are in the middle of a conversation, it is easier to remember words you have *heard* rather than words you have read). Now and then, especially the first few times you talk with native speakers, you may be stuck for words: you have an idea on your mind but the words just will not come out... When that happens, the above technique will help also. It puts you in the dynamic of using words you know, trying to place them and turns the conversation into something of a game, even when you are just getting started.

- **Work on your voice and breathing.** Use a deep, resonant, voice tone. Take the time to breathe deeply and to speak slowly. The air is your fuel. If you are out of breath, you cannot speak anymore. Speaking with a steady voice makes people listen and take notice. This is the sort of things you can work on in yoga, voice training, and singing classes. Basically, let the air flow down your body, as if filling your stomach (though, technically, this simply lets the air fill your lungs further down, lowering your diaphragm). This is the proper way to breathe and this is how babies breathe, actually. For now, keep in mind that good breathing and a good voice will help you communicate better while, at the same time, help you relax and energize.

The tips on mentioning people's accents and being spontaneous might not be usable to such an extent in a formal work setting. This is why it is a good idea to go out and practice in your own spare time first, for fun. If you really have to meet your first English speakers at work, then replace the above tips with making people repeat, to ensure your understanding, and jotting down ideas on a piece of paper. Later on, decide if you want to mention what you wrote down or not. In a work setting, try to be relaxed also and keep in mind that understanding each other is even more important there. It is perfectly alright to clarify things by asking people to repeat themselves.

Overall, meeting people in English is the chance to reap the benefits of what you have worked on so hard! Enjoy the moment. Enjoy the process. You will learn a few things doing so and will feel pretty good about yourself! (You are finally speaking with native speakers – *Yeah!*)

Later on, as you get back to your daily practice (TV shows, audio books, reading…) you will have **a new perspective on English**, earned from exposing yourself to the "real thing."

From now on, you should divide your time between practice and meeting people. Both activities will feed and improve upon one another. It is like sharpening a saw. Meeting people makes you want to practice more. Practicing more prepares you to talk to people even more easily, making you crave for more. As such, alternating between the two is critical.

WRAPPING IT UP

❖ Be proactive in finding native speakers. Big cities help and traveling makes everything possible.

❖ For work or for fun, on the phone or in person: prepare yourself. Be able to fix a date and clarify details.

❖ Most importantly, enjoy yourself meeting new people. Relax, try to be open and go out with a positive attitude. When talking to people, listen to them, be spontaneous and let your words flow.

Chapter 10

Thinking in English

What we think, we become

"One tongue, one person. Two tongues, two persons"
– Chinese proverb

GOAL & EXIT

Goal

Your goal is to think in English. It means two things:

- Visualizing ideas in your head and being able to turn them into English words right away, without relying on your native language at any point.
- Being able to entertain your inner dialogue in English, instead of in your native language.

Exit

You have reached your goal once you are able to do the two above items and are able to do so, on a regular basis. An example of this skill is to be able to think about a specific topic at length, in English. You should also be able to think about any topic, even if just basically, in English.

Both phenomenon should happen at will (you want to think in English) and on their own (ideas come to you in English, as you go about your day).

LOOKING INSIDE YOU

Thinking is a process we all do but we usually do not stop and examine how we do it. Cognitive science and behavioral psychology now give us more insight on how we think. Let us talk about it a little in order to gain more insight on how we think and how our brains work.

Dictionaries give us typically quite a few definitions of the verb "to think," with several variants. What they all have in common is that they always refer to thinking as the act of *bringing things to life in our own mind.*

We can all think in different ways, which have to do with our senses (the five senses: sight, hearing, taste, smell and touch; but also additional senses such as the perception of time and space), our ability to talk (our voice, others'), our feelings, our logic and our memory. We are also able to mix all of the above.

For example, we can think the following things:

• Remember a childhood memory, such as the first time we went to school. We might remember what it looked like. We might even remember what the school desk felt like (Was it wood? Plastic?). Or the voice of our teacher. Or even the smell of the classroom or the taste of the food at lunch. Those senses vary for everyone.

• Think of our next holidays and where we want to go. We might visualize the beautiful place where we want to go. Or what it will feel like visiting the place. Or what it will feel like to be relaxing on the beach. We might even imagine right now the feeling of walking barefoot in the sand.

• Think back of a conversation we have had with a friend or colleague. We can remember the words spoken, the voice tone and the laughs. That, of course, is in addition to the appearance of the place, and so on.

• We may even think of complex structures mostly based on logic, the way a programmer or a mathematician might.

We do have many ways available for us to think.

Also, note that some of those ways *have* to do with language (voices, conversations) while others *do not* (visualizations, touch, smell, etc.). Basically, it means you have language-based memories and other memories that are nonverbal, based on something else (visuals, memories of touch, smells, etc.).

So how can you start thinking in English?

Well, one very simple trick to help you think in English is for you to gain more memories of speech and conversations in English. This is what watching TV and movies, in English, without foreign subtitles, does (you create new memories you can think back on). It is also what listening to audio books does. It is also what meeting native speakers does. **All those activities create memories which are 100% in English.** This is one of the main benefits of applying the techniques described in this book. It forms a resource in which to draw when you want to express yourself. By having the experience, you can remember phrases that will be useful in your own conversations. The good thing about ideas is that they also have a life of their own: they come back to you often and make you think about them, without you always knowing why. So, **the more ideas you are exposed to in English, the more ideas will come back to you in that language**.

As for the forms of thinking that are not language-based (visualizations, touch, smell, etc.), **you need to be able to translate them into your own English words** when you want to talk about them. For example, if you want to share a memory with an English-speaking friend, you need to know the words to describe that memory. How do you do that? You need the vocabulary to describe your thoughts, along with the grammar skills to structure your words and finally, the phonetics skills to express your words out loud properly… and, of course, a little experience in order to do all that, at the same time, smoothly. You also need to stop the reflex you may have to speak in your native language. Words need to come on their own, in English.

For example, let us say you want to describe in English the first time you went to school. You may have told the story a dozen times before throughout your life, in your native language, obviously. When you want to tell the story again, in English, you need to *stop* the words from coming in your native language. Words may come to you in your native language because they always have, nothing more. You just need to stop that. How do you do that? You go slow and see that you have the option to use a *different* language any time you want. Of course, this is slow at first. This is like training a new muscle into being stronger or more flexible. You need regular practice to get it into shape: same thing with languages. Additionally, the more experience you have gained (through exposure to the language, with TV, meetings, *etc.*) the quicker it will become easy for you.

For the above example, as you think of your childhood memory, you would visualize, in your mind's eye, what the school looked like. If you have gained some vocabulary about buildings and/or school, describing it visually will be easy (you may remember words seen on TV or heard in books; this way, you are pretty sure how to pronounce them, too). As you want to describe your feelings on your first day at school, memories of people sharing such feelings in movies or in self-help books may come back to you. And so on with describing all the rest and telling your story. It is all based on associations: as you see things in your own mind, having seen the same or similar things before, in English, elsewhere, enables you to find your words. It happens almost automatically; words tend to come on their own.

Finally, you also have the case in which you want to talk about things that happened to you before *while* using your native language. For example, you want to talk, in English, about how you met your best friend and what you two talked about back then. You may then have to do two things: use the above technique (to turn visual thoughts into English words) and you may also need, for once, to translate (because you want to repeat, in English, some of the words you and your best friend said). This is a special case and is the only situation in which it is okay for you to translate from one language to another. The rest of the time, you should not use your native language at all but just try to **make your thoughts and English words match directly**, with no intermediary.

This may be a lot to take in one time. **In the coming days and weeks, you should take the time to *think about how you think*,** both in English and in your native language – compare the two. It will help you gain more control on the way you speak English and this will make switching from one language to the other, in your mind or in speech, much easier.

The next section gives you simple exercises for you to think in English.

Thinking in English: exercises

As we have seen, some thoughts are based on language, we call those verbal thoughts. Others are not based on language, we call those nonverbal thoughts. We will practice both, in English.

Developing verbal thoughts:

In this book, you have applied yourself to learning about subjects *you like* in English. You have learned through your reading, you have learned while listening to audio books. You have even learned, even if this is more relaxed, from watching TV.

What I would like you to do now is **write or talk** about those things:

- You favorite TV show and why you like it.

- The person you have had the most fun talking to in English, either online or in person: what happened and why it was so much fun.

- The topic you search the most on the Web and what it means to you or the audio book you have loved the most and what you have learned in it.

As you do that, either in writing or in conversation (you can do that on your own, or record yourself, or chat with someone), I want you to think in your own language the least possible, preferably not at all. Instead, when you are tempted to look for words in your own language, try to remember words and expressions you have heard or read during your experience with that TV show, person or topic. Also, if you do it in writing, try to think out loud in your mind, first.

The purpose of this exercise is to make you realize you

already have a wide set of resources available to you in English and that you have areas of expertise almost, that you feel comfortable talking about. The goal is also for you to see that you can use *strictly English*, nothing else, and still feel at ease.

Once you are done with this part of the exercise, here is the last step:

- Pick a random topic you know nothing about in English (this can be cars, cooking, an art, a place, whatever). Then pick a memory specifically about that topic. Examples: the time you had a flat tire, the last dish you cooked, an instrument you would like to pick up, a place you have heard about but never visited.

- Write or talk about that topic the same way you did in the previous exercise. It will be harder, still, try not to think in your native language at all. Instead, when you do not know a word or expressions, try describing what it looks like or using a different word. You may also describe it, as if asking for the word you are looking for. If you are doing the exercise with an English-speaking partner, try to have him tell you the word for it and check if you understood properly. Do not use the dictionary.

The purpose of this part of the exercise is to have you talk about a topic you are *not* familiar with and train you to still get away with it and still keep a good conversation going. You might be short for words at times, yet: you can still manage to express yourself and get to learn something out of the conversation.

The purpose is also for you to realize that the more exposed you are to a topic, in English, the easier it gets. As such, in order to become a great English speaker (and a great speaker in general, regardless of the language), you should try and get interested in all sorts of topics. Curiosity will feed your English immensely.

Develop non-verbal thoughts into words

As their name implies, non-verbal thoughts are not connected to any language. As such, what you need to practice is your ability to turn non-verbal thoughts into appropriate English words.

As such, you need to associate non-verbal thoughts (mental pictures, sounds, tastes, smells, feels and feelings) to their English words.

In order to do so, you should keep learning visually (TV shows and other video medias help here) and, also, you need to learn about feelings and the vocabulary around them (audio books and self-help usually help in this area).

Practice those exercises for two weeks, at least one day out of two. Vary the topics you think and talk about, day after day. You may practice them as you go out and meet native speakers or practice them on your own. Also practice this exercise in a more casual way, for a few months, as you go out, by telling stories or sharing memories.

TRANSLATING

I often discourage people from translating, mostly because **translating is not speaking.** When you want to talk with an English speaker, you want to be able to do so smoothly, and a prerequisite to do that is to turn your thoughts *directly* into English. As seen above, do not go through your native language first and then translate; this would be a really bad habit and a major waste of time.

However, if you need to translate for work or for someone who does not speak English, here is how to do it:

- First, work with whole sentences, not just words. (Remember: a word does not mean much of anything taken out of context. Or rather: a word can mean *too many* different things when taken out of context.) It will help you gain an overall understanding of where the translation will be going.

- Break down the sentence into smaller phrases, where each phrase makes sense on its own. The goal is for you to both detect idioms and work with something more manageable than a long sentence. It may seem to contradict the previous point but does not: you wanted the whole sentence first to get some overview and make sure you can translate accurately; now, you want to get into the specifics.

- Go through the sentence phrase by phrase and try to see what it evokes mentally. The goal here is to *turn words into thoughts*. You should see pictures or other similar thoughts in your mind at this point. It is like you are leaving the words world to go further up, into the "thoughts" world.

- Go through each thought you have in your mind and try transforming it into words in your destination language.

By doing so, you are able to translate accurately, by getting a sense of what the person actually wanted to say, getting the "feel and picture" for it, and then turning it into something really meaningful in the destination language.

In this translating process, your job is also to be accurate and truthful to the original. This is of course all especially true if you need to translate something for work.

It is usually easier to translate from English to our native language because we are then much more confident on how to say things than we would be trying to render anything and everything into proper English. (For this reason, professional translators traditionally only translate to their native language.)

THE RIGHT TIME TO THINK IN ENGLISH

A word of warning: thinking in English requires a certain knowledge and experience of the language. If you have skimmed through this book, not applying the exercises and practices described in it, chances are you will not feel comfortable thinking in English at all, all especially if this is your first foreign language. If that is the case: I strongly advise against applying this chapter right away as trying to think in English too early is counter-productive. The best time for you to start thinking in English is when you know a lot about constructing sentences, the way to pronounce English and when you master about at least *one* specific topic in English. If you are not there yet, go back to the previous chapters until you have reached the exit goals. Enjoy your practice by committing yourself to each chapter and thoughts will start to pop up in English on their own.

WRAPPING IT UP

❖ Take time to *think about how you think*. The goal is for you to realize that some of your thoughts are language-based (verbal) while others are not (nonverbal).

❖ Practice the *Thinking in English exercises* for two weeks, at least one day out of two or more.

❖ Also practice the *Thinking in English exercises* in conversation when you meet people, for at least 3 months, by talking about various topics and talking about some of your memories.

What next?

Epilogue and your next steps

"If I had eight hours to chop down a tree, I'd spend six sharpening my axe."
– Abraham Lincoln

First of all, thank you for buying this book. It is not always easy telling people that they actually have to pick up new habits to achieve the success they want, so thank you for listening to me and reading this book. Most importantly: congratulations for actually taking action and applying the content of this book! Ideas are easy to read about, it is applying them that does take some courage.

As you have kept applying the principles described here, you must have reached some new level of fluency and ease in English. Everyone's story is different. Would you be so kind to share yours with me? You can write me at this address:

fabien.snauwaert@gmail.com
Put "SUCCESS STORY" in the subject. Those are the e-mails I read first.

You may now be wondering what to do regarding your English. First of all, the most important step is for you to **keep your current level**. Losing it may come quickly, especially if you made a lot of progress really fast. The best and easiest way to maintain and expand on your current level is to keep listening to audio books. By doing so, you will keep learning about new topics you are passionate about, you will keep hearing and thinking about those words and, quite conveniently, you can do that from the comfort of any MP3, at home, in transportation or anywhere else. No time lost.

The second thing I would like you to do is to expose yourself to more and more accents. You may have grown accustomed to specific accents and they may even start to feel like a part of you. However, in order to have a broad view and to build your confidence further, I strongly suggest you go and look for accents you are not used to. The American accents are by far the easiest to expose yourself to but being comfortable with the various British accents is quite an asset, especially if you live in Europe, and it is better to grow used to them.

Finally, I strongly advise you keep practicing all of the techniques described in this book. They are not here just to give you a quick boost in English. They are here to give you a huge, continuous and renewed experience of the English language. How good your English is really depends on how exposed to it you have been. The habits you have started adopting are the best and easiest to use to gain a lot of experience, day after day. As such, keep the habit of looking for things on the Internet in English, keep the habit of watching TV in English without subtitles, same thing for movies and keep the habit of meeting new people. Meet them in person if you can. In smaller cities, do it online! A world of opportunities awaits you. You can now speak the language with ease; you are only at the beginning of your journey. From there, you can now go anywhere you like.

Enjoy the journey!

Fabien Snauwaert
Paris, France 2010.

Books made into movies

Great books into great movies

These are books for all tastes, just pick the movie you have liked the most and read the novel.

A Beautiful Mind

A Clockwork Orange

Alice in Wonderland

Angels & Demons

Black Hawk Down

Bladerunner / Do Androids Dream of Electric Sheep?

Blow

Bridget Jone's Diary

Brokeback Mountain

Charlie and the Chocolate Factory

Chronicles of Narnia

Curious Case of Benjamin Button, The

Fight Club

Gangs of New York

I Am Legend

I, Robot

Into the Wild

Jarhead

Kiss, Kiss, Bang, Bang / Bodies Are Where You Find Them

Lord of the Rings, The

Million Dollar Baby / Rope Burns: Stories from the Corner

Minority Report

Misery

P.S. I Love You

Ripley's Game

Shutter Island

Slumdog Millionaire / Q&A

The Bourne Identity

The Da Vinci Code

The Godfather

The Pianist

The Prestige

The Pursuit of Happyness

The Talented Mr. Ripley

Time Machine, The

Twilight

War of the Worlds

For more suggestions, you can visit "Based on the Book" [http://www.mcpl.lib.mo.us/readers/movies/], a compilation of over a thousand books that have been made into films.

Recommended sitcoms

Popular and quality situational comedies

Here is a list of sitcoms you can trust to have a laugh and improve your English. Of course, tastes vary, so try and check them out for yourself on Yo u Tub e or similar before you buy.

I have selected them based on how fun they are but also on how long they have been running.

- Ally McBeal (1997–2002, 5 seasons)
- It's Always Sunny in Philadelphia (2005–present; 6 seasons)
- The Big Bang Theory (2007–present, 4 seasons)
- Friends (1994–2004, 10 seasons)
- How I Met Your Mother (2005–present, 6 seasons)
- Malcolm In The Middle (2000–2006, 7 seasons)
- Married… with Children (1987–1997, 11 seasons)
- The Nanny (1993–1999, 6 seasons)
- The Office (2005–present, 6 seasons)
- Scrubs (2001–2010, 9 seasons)
- Seinfeld (1989–1998, 9 seasons)
- Sex and the City (1998–2004, 6 seasons)

Watching American and British TV from abroad

TV without borders

There are several ways to get live American and British TV from abroad. Here is an overview of your current options.

VPN SYSTEMS

Several services now allow you to watch TV replays online for free. The most famous service in this category is Hulu:

> http://www.hulu.com

The only bad thing is... At the time of writing, you need to be located in the US to use such services!

The good news is, technically, you can sign up to what is called a VPN system: this is a computer located in the US that will allow you to pretend that you are indeed located in the US.

You simply sign up for a VPN system in the US and then you can use Hulu and other similar services.

Here are a couple of companies that provide such a service:

> http://www.adtelly.tv
> http://www.vpngates.com

Try them before you sign up for the long-term, as their quality also depends from where you are located (if you are too far from their servers, world-wide, you might have a bad connection; this varies from company to company).

Some companies may or may not tolerate the use of VPNs to access their services. Check their terms and conditions.

PLACESHIFTING

The Slingbox

Placeshifting is the practice of watching to media broadcasted by a remote device. Example: you are in Spain but access a TV system located in the USA. How do you do that? There are now devices designed just for that. The best example is the Slingbox:

http://www.slingbox.com

This is a device you connect to a TV setup (cable box, satellite receiver, recorder…) and to your Internet connection. By doing so, you can then watch that TV from anywhere in the world.

The only thing is… You actually need to have a TV and a Slingbox connected together somewhere in the United States or in the United Kingdom for it to work!

Slingbox rental companies

Several businesses now provide Slingbox rental services. The most famous one is a2btv:

http://www.a2btv.com

They have a free offer to try their service out and their support staff is quite helpful in my experience. I suggest you try it out to see how good of a signal you get (again, the quality may vary depending on your location).

SATELLITE TV

For the satellite option to work, you need to be in an area covered by the satellites that broadcast American, British or Australian TV.

If you already own a satellite dish, I think this is a good option and you can start receiving some decent TV channels even without a monthly fee.

OTHER

Digital television

Digital terrestrial television may have made new channels available in your country. You may find English-speaking channels there, however, typically, those will only be news channels. For traditional channels, you will need one of the methods described here.

Legal downloads

You might want to try iTunes or similar video download services. At the time of writing, however, newest releases on such sites were only available to people residing in the U.S. – in which case, a VPN system could be a solution; check their terms and services.

Bibliography

Awaken The Giant Within
Anthony Robbins, Free Press
A great self-help book, to help you complete things in time and with passion, as well as follow your dreams.

How To Learn Any Language
Barry Farber, Citadel Press Book
A great and rare book. The author shares his personal experience as a polyglot and also provides many tips to help acquire and memorize a new language.

How To Develop a Super-Power Memory
Harry Lorayne, A. Thomas & Co. Preston
A great book on improving one's memory, written by a genius on the topic. May be hard to find nowadays; instead, you might want to try **The Memory Book** by the same author.

The 7 Habits of Highly Effective People
Stephen R. Covey, Franklin Covey Co.
A great self-help and business book, to help you get organized, both in your personal life and in business.

What To Say When You Talk To Yourself
Shad Helmstetter, Pocket Books
A great self-help book, this book is also, due to its subject, the chance to get more and more into the habit of thinking in English.

Table of content

Made in the USA
Lexington, KY
07 July 2012